WHITE-COLLAR WORK

CAMBRIDGE STUDIES IN SOCIOLOGY

Editors: R. M. Blackburn and K. Prandy

This series presents research findings of theoretical significance on subjects of social importance. It allows a wide variety of topics and approaches, though central themes are provided by economic life and social stratification. The format ranges from monographs reporting specific research to sets of original research papers on a common theme. The series is edited in Cambridge and contains books arising mainly from work carried out there. However, suitable books, wherever they originate, are included.

Published

R. M. Blackburn and Michael Mann
THE WORKING CLASS IN THE LABOUR MARKET

K. Prandy, A. Stewart and R. M. Blackburn
WHITE-COLLAR WORK

A. Stewart, K. Prandy and R. M. Blackburn
SOCIAL STRATIFICATION AND OCCUPATIONS

Forthcoming

K. Prandy, A. Stewart and R. M. Blackburn
WHITE-COLLAR UNIONISM

Also by K. Prandy

PROFESSIONAL EMPLOYEES

Also by R. M. Blackburn

UNION CHARACTER AND SOCIAL CLASS
PERCEPTIONS OF WORK (*with H. Beynon*)

White-Collar Work

K. Prandy, A. Stewart
and R. M. Blackburn

© K. Prandy, A. Stewart and R. M. Blackburn 1982

First published 1982 by
THE MACMILLAN PRESS LTD
London and Basingstoke
Companies and representatives
throughout the world

ISBN 0 333 24331 5 (hardcover)
ISBN 0 333 33273 3 (paperback)

Printed in Great Britain by
PITMAN PRESS
Bath

Contents

List of Tables and Figures

TABLES

FIGURES

Preface

The study reported in this book is part of the sociological research programme of the Department of Applied Economics in the University of Cambridge. The original project was financed by the Social Science Research Council, whose support we should like to acknowledge with gratitude.

Survey research is ultimately made possible only by the willing co-operation of those who are interviewed, and so our major thanks must go to the many whose responses constitute the greater part of this work. We should also like to thank those responsible in the employing establishments – of which there are rather too many to be named individually – who gave not only their permission for the interviews to be carried out, but also their time and help in other ways.

Large-scale research is also a team effort, and the authors reporting the results depend very substantially on the support provided by many others. One person deserves special mention. In the early part of the analysis, especially, before the easy availability of program packages, we were given invaluable help and advice by Dr Joyce Wheeler. Among other things she produced for us a program (SORDENS) to carry out the disorderly interlocking referred to in Chapter 2. In addition we extend our thanks in general terms to all those who helped make the research and its reporting possible – from the interviewers who collected the data and those who helped work on it by offering their statistical and computing skills to those who provided typing, secretarial and general administrative services.

1 Work Inequality: Response and Reproduction

The middle class has long held a fascination for sociologists. For some its existence is a demonstration of the superiority of Weber's insights, concerning the importance of status, over those of Marx. For others, who reject such a view, it is nevertheless a problem: most of its members are, like manual workers, propertyless and obliged to sell their labour power; yet many of them, unlike manual workers, fail to behave in the ways that the basic theory predicts for such propertyless workers. It is not surprising that they have attracted much attention, nor that interest is growing as the non-manual section of the labour force becomes ever larger, and at the same time apparently more militant. Some have seen in these developments portents for the future of industrial societies, with non-manual workers forming the new working class or at least a dominant part of a (largely 'middle-class') proletariat. Indeed they are right to some extent, since this is a key area of social change. However, we believe that most accounts are too simple, and an adequate understanding of these important issues calls for a much more rigorous analysis than has previously been attempted.

We shall avoid use of the term 'middle class' because of its unsatisfactory nature as a conceptual entity. The choice of non-manual employees, from supervisors and clerks to professionals and senior managers, as the subject of our study clearly indicates the area of our concern, but we start with no assumption of 'class' unity or distinctiveness. By focusing on this section of the labour force the research is designed to examine variations within it, rather than to compare it with other sectors of society. However, social variations must be understood in their wider social context, and in seeking to explain their sources we have attempted to construct a general model which is applicable beyond the limited group studied. At the start we spent a considerable time working out the theoretical model which has guided the investigation and determining what information would be needed. In doing this we paid particular attention to problems of measurement and especially to the relation between measurement and theory. It was not always possible, of course, to obtain the sort of measures we would have liked. Nevertheless the report is based on an extensive, systematic analysis of an unusually comprehensive range of data.

The aim of the present chapter is largely to describe our thinking in the early stages of the research. To some extent we have been unable to avoid presenting the theoretical discussion in a way that reflects later changes in our ideas. Nevertheless, at this stage we believe it desirable to present the argument in such a manner as to bring out the basic features of the theoretical approach which actually inspired the empirical research. It is only in this way that the latter is fully comprehensible.

Our original concern was with variations in trade unionism, which also reflects the importance of the issue of class in our thinking. However, while this has remained the major focus, it became clear as we elaborated our theoretical ideas on that topic that it needed to be set within a wider context covering a number of different forms of behaviour undertaken by people in employing organisations. In consequence, our approach will appear to diverge from the traditional concerns of class analysis, and it is therefore important to indicate in general terms why we believe that divergence to be justified. The arguments will be elaborated, and the relevance of the divergence argued, in the concluding chapter. At a practical level these developments led to a useful division of emphasis in our analysis, so that we present our findings in two volumes. In this book we are concerned with variations in the way work is experienced and the different forms of adaptations and outcomes. While this includes the desire for union representation and preferences with regard to its character, the analysis of involvement in actual organisations is undertaken in a subsequent volume (*White-Collar Unionism*). There we shall be able to give more attention to the contextual influences which are clearly of particular importance in the case of collective action. The second book also takes up and develops the arguments introduced at the end of this volume.

Since our analysis is concerned with individuals it begins by taking as given one of the major concerns of class analysis, that is to say the structure of inequalities of various kinds and the mechanisms by which this is created and maintained. Our approach begins by seeing these inequalities as leading to variations in individual or group experience which assume a patterned form in so far as they are shared with others. Individuals react, positively or negatively, to these experiences, but they do so by making them comprehensible. Thus their responses are not simply reactive, they are also active, given that their future behaviour depends upon their understanding of their experiences. However, their understanding is likely to be firmly bound within limits set by their normal experience. Our original emphasis on trade unionism involved seeing this as a strategy pursued, or at least desired, by individuals as a means of changing an undesirable situation. Its consequences, if successful, were then a change in the structure of inequalities. That is to say, individual or group behaviour, resulting from particular sets of experiences, is involved in the changed reproduction of the system.

In developing this we were concerned mainly with other possible individual reactions to undesirable situations. We refer to these as adaptations or strategies, although we do not see them as necessarily consciously pursued, any more than the comprehensions upon which they are based are necessarily, or even typically, consciously articulated. Nevertheless, some have the external appearance of strategies, in so far as they have the consequence of adapting the situation, or of adapting the individual to it. However, these different forms of behaviour – or more usually in this volume attitudinal predispositions – should not be seen only in terms of their individual consequences. They should also be seen in terms of the way in which they serve either to reinforce the situation in which experience occurs, and thus to reproduce the existing structure of inequalities in unchanged form, or to contribute towards change. There is not a one-to-one correspondence between individual and aggregate outcomes. In particular, for example, promotion can be seen at one level as a strategy to change the individual's situation, but at another as part of a process which constitutes a reproducing system.

Our concern, then, is at the outset with the differential distribution of different kinds of rewards. Our approach leads us, first, to specifying these rewards; second, to considering the levels of the rewards that individuals received, or saw themselves as receiving; third, to trying to assess the expectations that individuals had with respect to each; and fourth, to examining the relationship between these perceptions and expectations and predisposition towards different strategies.

EXPECTATIONS

It is scarcely novel to treat human beings as reward-seeking, but a major problem has always been that such an approach has tended to lead either to tautology, in that any goal pursued can be understood as a reward, or to vagueness, in that no simple formulation can cover the wide variety of goals and rewards that people pursue, or both. The present treatment attempts to avoid these problems by specifying in advance a limited range of rewards that individuals seek at work, but a possible consequence of this has been a neglect of other significant rewards, or perhaps a too-narrow definition of the nature of a particular reward. We have also tried to avoid another of the pitfalls of this approach, the danger of psychological reductionism. Our intention is to be explicit about psychological assumptions, but to treat expectations from a sociological point of view – that is, to try to hypothesise about those determinants of expectation which are related to social experience and social location.

There are a variety of general models that one can adopt in seeing individuals as reward-seeking. Some emphasise optimisation within a set of rewards (e.g. Marshall, 1920; Blau, 1964), while others posit a structure of psychological needs (e.g. Maslow, 1954; Zetterberg, 1962). However, quite apart from any internal weaknesses, all such models face a problem in specifying the relationship between general motivation and the rewards sought in employment. To a large extent, in the past the problem has either been ignored or has been assumed away by postulating the over-riding importance of one particular need. The usual picture of 'economic man', for example as portrayed by Taylor (1947), does not allow him a concern at work with anything much more than the size of his pay-packet, but on the other hand it rarely tells us anything about his behaviour outside of work. In the case of Mayo (1945), however, and to a lesser extent the Human Relations school which developed out of his work, it is clear that the need, or perhaps needs, for belongingness and esteem were not only the prime motivators within the employment situation, but also outside it.

Attempts to demonstrate the over-riding importance of one particular reward as a motivator in the employment situation have the advantage of conceptual economy, but they have failed. Indeed, the partial success of each has made it clear that a variety of rewards must be considered. Those writers who have recognised this fact have tended to follow one of two paths, either simply to suggest several, perhaps with some indication of their relative importance but with an assumption of homogeneity of motivation, or to hypothesise about possible differences in motivation.

The first path is clearly more straightforward, but is also less interesting. For this reason it has had less appeal, so that even those studies which have adopted the simple expedient of asking workers about the different rewards that they derive from their work have also made some attempt to consider differences between, for example, skill or status groups (e.g. Friedmann and Havighurst, 1954; Morse and Weiss, 1955). In part, of course, since this approach is concerned with rewards actually secured in work, differences will reflect what is differentially available, rather than what is differentially desired. At the least one can say that the two are likely to be confused. A somewhat different line, which assumes homogeneity of workers, but which distinguishes between types of rewards, as either satisfiers ('motivators') or dissatisfiers ('hygiene' or 'maintenance' factors), has been taken by Herzberg (1968).

A far more promising approach, and the one that we have adopted, has been to accept that workers may differ in the kinds of rewards that they seek at work. However, if vagueness and circularity are to be avoided, it is essential that some attempt is made to explain these differences, rather than simply to take them as given. In addition it is important to distinguish between differences in the relative importance of various rewards and differences in the actual level of expectations regarding those rewards. For example, the fact that one group of workers places greater emphasis on money than does another group does not imply that their level of expectations regarding earnings is higher, and indeed the opposite may well be the case.

An important variant on the theme of the heterogeneity of motives is to be found in the work of Goldthorpe and his associates (Goldthorpe, 1966; Goldthorpe *et al.*, 1968). They have tended to stress the operation of the labour market as a mechanism for allocating workers with particular orientations (for example, primary emphasis on pecuniary rewards) to jobs and firms which offer the most appropriate 'mix' of rewards. Thus they argue both that there will be a relatively high degree of homogeneity within a firm, and also that, for example with respect to assembly-line work, apparent deprivations will not necessarily be of significance to the individual worker. In fact subsequent research (Blackburn and Mann, 1979) has shown that for manual workers the labour market allows very little scope for choice in accordance with orientations, and for the most part the workers have less clearly defined orientations than suggested by Goldthorpe and his colleagues. No similar study has been made of the situation for non-manual workers.

The primary concern of Goldthorpe *et al.* (1968) was with instrumentalism, an emphasis on pecuniary rewards. One particularly significant aspect of their explanation was that individuals who are downwardly socially mobile compared to their fathers (or immobile compared to upward-moving siblings) feel the need to maintain their absolute or relative material standard of living. This is valuable as an explicit recognition of the significance of reference groups, or more broadly social referents, in the determination of expectations. Despite the increasing evidence for the existence of social comparison processes since their first elaboration by Merton and Kitt (1952), little attention has been paid to them as determinants of expectations at work and even less to the problem of predicting significant social referents. There are important exceptions to this last statement, in particular Lipset and Trow (1957), who consider the choice of comparisons made by trade unions in formulating wage claims, and Form and Geschwender (1962) who compare the individual's position with that of his father and brothers (though, unlike Goldthorpe *et al.* (1968) they see the reference as an explanation of dissatisfaction with the job rather than instrumentalism).

There is, however, some evidence (Bonjean, Bruce and Williams, 1967) that the family is not a significant basis for social reference among non-manual workers. An alternative view would stress, not present comparisons, but processes that shape expectations, such as habituation to a particular level through early socialisation. For non-manual workers, particularly, experience of career advancement leads to an upward revision of expectations. While one need not accept Durkheim's extreme argument (1952, 247) that because 'a more awakened reflection suggests better conditions', then 'capacity for feeling is in itself an insatiable and bottomless abyss', there is good evidence that success raises expectations (see Atkinson, 1964, 258–67). Such a process would operate in the opposite direction to that of social comparison.

In summary, then, we decided, firstly, to concentrate our attention on five types of rewards that are sought, at least by a significant number of workers, in the employment situation. For purposes of analysis, they are presented under the broad headings of income, security, status, social relationships and intrinsic job rewards. However, we are aware of elements of diversity within their composition – the last, for example, includes such matters as control, variety and use of abilities.

Secondly, we would anticipate that there are several characteristics of individuals, relating to their social background and experience, that would influence the nature of their orientations towards work. A full discussion of the nature of orientations, and their twin aspects of salience and expectations, must be postponed to Chapter 4. For the present we shall note simply that orientations involve both the importance of the various rewards, primarily the five listed above, and their expected levels. Moreover, these expectations should be understood as being what individuals feel themselves as 'reasonably' entitled to get, and not necessarily either what they want or what they may realistically anticipate getting.

The clearest point that emerges from the discussion is that personal experience of advantage is likely to lead to higher expectations of all five types of reward, but especially those of income, status and intrinsic job. Such experience may arise in early upbringing or through later career success (thus producing complexities in causal relationships). Additionally, expectations may be raised as a result either of social comparison – with, for example, higher-status neighbours and friends – or of socialisation, particularly that associated with education. Higher levels of the latter, especially, are likely to be associated with greater expectations regarding intrinsic job rewards.

The converse of the argument that success is associated with higher expectations is that continued experience of a level of rewards below that expected is likely to lead to a downward revision of expectations. Thus, older respondents who have not experienced improvement will tend to exhibit lower levels than those at an earlier stage of their working life.

REWARDS

So far we have considered only the question of the rewards that individuals seek at work, and have said nothing about their availability. The actual level of rewards enjoyed by our respondents is an empirical question for later investigation, but we clearly have to recognise the importance of work as a means by which rewards are allocated to individuals. Not only is income from employment the basis for life outside work, but employment locates the worker within an internal hierarchy, and the actual job tasks involve, in varying quantities, the other rewards that we have discussed. Moreover, there is a clear structure to the distribution of rewards, in particular a tendency for them to vary together rather than independently. Thus those with higher incomes tend also to enjoy a higher occupational status, a greater opportunity for self-actualisation in their work, greater security and the potential, at least, for developing social relationships.

The other important aspect of the availability of rewards is that of access to experience in the structure of reward distribution. There is considerable evidence, which our own results substantiate, that benefits are differentially available to those of different social backgrounds. Thus one major reason for investigating the relationship between, particularly, individuals' 'ascribed status' by virtue of their family of origin, their educational attainment and their occupational experience is to try to disentangle the effects of present social location and of social background.

As may have been apparent already in the earlier discussion, it is very difficult to discuss expectations separately from rewards. For example, there is the question of whether work is a significant area for the satisfaction of all the needs that might be assumed to motivate individuals. While one can hardly doubt that the presence of various rewards in the employment situation would positively contribute to overall satisfaction, even if only to a small extent, a good deal of controversy surrounds the question of whether the absence of certain rewards would be of any psychological significance (see, for example, Dubin, 1956; Kornhauser, 1965). An adequate answer to this problem cannot be given simply in terms of individuals' responses to questions designed to discover the rewards obtained from work, since these are to a large extent determined by what is actually available in the situation rather than by what may be desired. Even the distinction that was made above, between 'realistic' expectations, or anticipations, and expectations in the sense of wants, is likely to prove – at least in part – more conceptual than real, in so far as what is available to individuals will serve as some constraint on their wants. Whether it is possible to demonstrate the existence of more basic expectations, perhaps unarticulated or even unconscious, will depend on the success in formulating hypotheses relating the non-satisfaction of such wants to observable behavioural outcomes, a question which is taken up later. However, we may note that there is no *a priori* reason why workers should not seek any rewards from work that they would want elsewhere, and in so far as they do not it may be seen as resulting from the limitations of circumstances.

The other respect in which expectations and rewards cannot be clearly separated is in the question of frames of reference. It is possible that certain rewards, those related to 'physiological' needs and perhaps to self-actualisation, are in some sense absolute, but for the most part the rewards enjoyed, or missed, by individuals have meaning to them only in terms of the extent to which such rewards are available to others of whom they are aware. That is, except in limited, although perhaps very important, cases, the individual cannot be aware of deprivation or privilege absolutely, but only relatively. The comparative element is more apparent for some rewards than others: thus status rewards are explicitly relative, but it may be argued that enjoyment of income depends on what it will buy. However, the latter case is only pushing the relativity back to the buying, when individuals' expectations depend on the behaviour of others, and so on their incomes (or wealth). Clearly, therefore, their knowledge of what is available to others will be an important determinant of their perceptions of their own situations. However, for the most part such 'knowledge' is problematic, since it is individuals' perceptions of the rewards enjoyed by others which are significant, not the real situation – although the two are certainly related.

The process of comparison entails distinguishing the parties involved. Thus the development of expectations involves individuals in a perception of others as in some respect similar to or different from themselves (though the perception of significant difference always rests on some underlying assumption of similarity). Their expectations are then related either directly to the rewards of a perceived similar group or indirectly, through a conception of ordering and 'distance', to those of a different group. Of course, such comparisons may occur at different levels; for example, they may relate themselves both as individuals to a group that they define as similar, and as 'members' of this group to some other group.

The extent to which differences, especially those of a detrimental sort, are perceived, yet tolerated, will depend upon the cognitions which interpret these differences. Differences are integral to the understandings of social and economic systems and disaffection is likely to be the result of the disruption of standard differences rather than a consequence of such differences themselves. The greater the standard differences between groups the less likely are these groups to form important frames of reference for each other, although it is possible that disruptions of established patterns could be large enough to bring such comparisons to the fore.

Our research tries to examine how different frames of reference operate by getting the individual in most cases to assess his position relative to several groups. Firstly, there is his position as an individual relative to that of members of the same occupation, both within his own firm and in the wider society. We believe that for most people these will be the most important comparisons. Then there is his position, both as an individual and as one of an occupational group, relative to those in, for the most part, superior and inferior positions compared with his own. Ideally we would have wished a number of comparisons with groups at varying distances from each respondent, but this would have called for an extremely complex set of research procedures. We therefore took the simplest option and concentrated on one 'upward' (for most of our respondents) comparison with 'top managers', and one 'downward', with manual workers. In each case both an internal, company, and an external, wider society, frame of reference was provided.

JOB SATISFACTION AND COMMITMENT TO THE ORGANISATION

Having considered individuals as bringing certain expectations to their current employment, and the latter as providing them with various rewards which, to a greater or lesser degree, meet these expectations, we can regard their expressions of satisfaction as an indication of the extent to which this is the case. Thus we should find that satisfaction decreases with greater expectations and increases with higher rewards. As well as trying to determine the levels of satisfaction with each of the separate rewards, we can also consider the way in which these are resolved by the individual into an overall judgement of the job.

However, such expressions of satisfaction or dissatisfaction have to be interpreted with care. The way in which job satisfaction is typically conceptualised involves a strong element of voluntarism, in that an assumption of individuals' freedom of choice is generally made. Hence, 'satisfaction' is equated with 'liking' and 'happiness', for example. Furthermore, satisfaction is taken as indicating normative approval of whatever arrangements exist to allocate the rewards concerned. In particular, in the case of job satisfaction, it is assumed to indicate commitment to the employing organisation – its goals, authority structure and criteria for reward distribution. Such an assumption, based upon a lack of theoretical and conceptual clarity, is clearly problematic. To begin with, the causal relationship between satisfaction and commitment has rarely been specified. While it is possible to argue that to some extent the level of commitment influences the level of satisfaction, it seems much more plausible that the most important influence is in the reverse direction, from satisfaction to commitment, or at least that both result from the same organisational characteristics. In the first case the use of job satisfaction as an indicator of commitment amounts to using a 'cause' as a measure of an 'effect', in a situation where no causal relationship has in fact been demonstrated, while the second even fails to specify the cause. Either way a critical hypothesis has been assumed rather than put to the test.

Moreover, there are several grounds for doubting the strength of the relationship between satisfaction and commitment. In part, of course, the former may be determined by more general factors, such as individuals' acceptance or otherwise of particular occupations, and not solely by their experiences, or rewards, within the organisation. A more important point, though, is that job satisfaction alone is not sufficient, and both expectations and the level of rewards need also to be taken into account. Job satisfaction is a function of both expectations and rewards, but the influence of the latter is direct as well as indirect. For example, two individuals within the organisation may both express the same, low, level of satisfaction with their job, and let us assume for simplicity that in each case this reflects the same ratio of expectations to rewards. However, the individual with the higher level of rewards is more likely to be normatively committed to the organisation because, although he may be relatively dissatisfied, the present structure of reward distribution is more favourable to him than most alternatives. This is much less likely to be the case for the individual with a low level of rewards. His commitment will in addition depend on the extent to which he attributes his low rewards to the organisation, rather than to other factors (see Portes, 1971 for a discussion of the relation between satisfaction and structural blame).

As we have written of it here, commitment is to the employing organisation though in practice this will be difficult to separate from commitment to the form of employment. (Among employees with low levels of reward low commitment is likely to be both to the type of employment and to particular employers.) Those with high levels of rewards might feel aggrieved by the failure of their employers to grant the marginal increases they believe they are entitled to, but the disaffection need not involve a low level of commitment to the form of employment. Employees in that sort of situation are likely to be well aware of their general advantages even if their dissatisfaction is sufficient for them to seek employment elsewhere. To the extent that alternative employment is not available the two will be less easily distinguished.

Conversely, in the case of those who are relatively satisfied high commitment may be anticipated from those who enjoy a high level of rewards, but it is much more problematic for those with lower rewards. In large part, the basic problem lies in the meaning of satisfaction, and where high satisfaction is a consequence of low expectations it becomes very difficult to maintain our earlier distinction between expectations and anticipations. If low expectations are to some extent a result of low anticipations, then the meaning of 'satisfaction' becomes blurred, and the relationship between it and normative commitment consequently more problematic (see Kornhauser, 1965; Beynon and Blackburn, 1972).

Much the same difficulty of conceptualisation, and measurement, arises in considering the case where individuals have very low expectations at work with regard to particular types of reward. Whether it is possible for individuals to neglect certain rewards at work may be left as an open question, but even if they do so and, for example, emphasise financial rewards almost exclusively, it would seem less likely that this, as it were, partial and conditional satisfaction would lead to normative commitment to the same extent as a more general satisfaction. Etzioni (1961) seems to suggest just this point in distinguishing between utilitarian compliance, in conjunction with remunerative power, and normative compliance, in conjunction with normative power. In so far as he treats employing organisations as simple cases of authority based on remunerative power, he implies that normative compliance does not exist for 'lower' participants. On the other hand, though, he argues that their 'higher' participants do exhibit moral involvement. Unfortunately, there is no explanation offered of the genesis of such involvement, nor of why and at what level in the organisation the change begins to occur.

However, the important difference, of degree rather than of kind, would seem to be between those jobs at a lower level whose tasks are more tightly defined and thus where compliance can be more easily monitored and secured, and those at higher levels were the complexity or unpredictability of the work requires that more discretion be left to the individual worker. Since the requirements of the job are rather diffuse, 'compliance' with them is difficult to assess. Thus what is most needed from workers at these higher levels in the organiation is a relatively high degree of positive commitment, particularly as any attempt to limit their discretion by a more rigid specification and control of work would tend to contravene their expectations regarding self-actualisation. Such attempts may well be self-defeating – studies of bureaucracy, for example, have pointed to both the possibly harmful effects of rigid adherence to the rules, as with Merton's (1957) 'bureaucratic personality', and to the beneficial effects of breaking the rules, as with what Blau (1956) calls 'adjustive development'.

It would seem, therefore, that job satisfaction can be treated as a valid indicator of commitment only for those at the higher levels of employing organisations. Although it might be possible to conceive of measures of commitment which would be more direct, and valid, indicators a basic problem would remain. Such a measure would be primarily intended to tap the extent of conscious normative acceptance, but there is no *a priori* reason for allowing this primacy. On the contrary, there is a great deal to be said for treating the normative element as just one of a number of possible outcomes. This would imply the specification of other outcomes, particularly those which involve behaviour.

In doing this we shall be concerned with the individual's relationship to the employing organisation only indirectly, through the structure and processes of reward distribution. The concern with normative commitment or compliance has largely been motivated by a desire to solve the 'problems' created for employers when they are lacking, and which may be manifested in low productivity, absenteeism or turnover, for example. Our approach is to concentrate on individuals and the practical problems that may be created for them by their experience within the structure of reward distribution. For some, such problems will be few – their experience will be largely consonant with their understanding. For others, however, this will not be so, and individuals will adapt, or adapt to, their situation. The result will tend to be a resolution of the discrepancy between their expectations and the rewards available to them.

Behaviour, however, does not only serve to maintain or change the individual's situation. In so far as it is patterned it also contributes to the reproduction of society. It may do so in such a way as to reinforce existing processes and arrangements, or in a way that tends to bring about change, particularly in the distribution of rewards. The links between the two levels are complex, and there is certainly no one-to-one relationship between maintenance or change at the individual and at the collective level. Some previous theories have concentrated on the question of maintenance, but have seen it primarily as a question of normative integration. Interestingly, traditional class and conflict theories have largely ignored this aspect, and have tended to emphasise change. Both, however, have underplayed the significance of rewards and the circumstances in which expectations are generated, assuming either a natural harmony of interests on the one hand, or a basic conflict on the other.

ADAPTATIONS

At the basic level we postulate that individuals whose level of rewards does not match up to their expectations will either seek to avoid their situation by withdrawal from it, or will adapt it or themselves in some way so as the reduce the discrepancy (cf. Argyris, 1957; Merton, 1957, chs 4, 5). Withdrawal is most clearly exhibited in leaving – permanent avoidance of the organisation, and in promotion – movement to a new and more favourable position within the reward hierarchy. It may also be manifested in temporary forms, as in absenteeism. Perhaps equally, or more, significant examples are those associated with the various forms of mental or emotional avoidance, such as day-dreaming, the retreat into apathy, ritualism, or the rather elusive idea which is generally taken to be central to the concept of alienation, that of the instrumental use of the physical self without the involvement of the mental, or real, self.

The processes of adaptation to situations of deprivation may occur over very long periods of time and may start long before entry to employment. While such adaptation is still a process of resolving discrepancies between expectations and rewards we may not be able to capture the principal elements of the process in a survey of employees. In some cases we will see its effects by comparing people differently located in the process (for example, we can show a downward adjustment of expectations with age and an associated rise in psychological withdrawal and self-estrangement). However, in other cases the processes will not be themselves visible, but will only appear as completed adjustments associated with aspects of respondents' backgrounds and past experiences.

Adaptation of a situation, what is in a sense a more positive form of avoidance, can also take relatively temporary or permanent forms, although the degree of institutionalisation and formalisation of the adaptation expresses the difference more adequately. In each case there is involved the subversion of organisational goals, authority structure, regulations and so on; but with permanent, or institutionalised, adaptation there is the important difference that in addition to changes in the distribution of rewards there are also changes in the distribution of power, and more particularly of authority, and so in the capacity for control over the distribution of rewards. Thus, although it may be possible for individuals to affect the rewards available to them, either by altering their side of the effort bargain by lessening their effort or by increasing their sense of power and control by outwitting supervisors and breaking rules, nevertheless these activities are still treated as 'illegal' within the system and may be countered by sanctions. Permanent restructuring of the situation is more likely to involve the development of special institutions, and eventually new definitions of legality and of legitimate use of sanctions. In the latter case particularly, but to some extent in all cases of adaptation, problems of feedback begin to enter into any analysis. In the first place an increase in rewards may lead to greater satisfaction, and secondly the organisation, with its authority and reward distribution structure, is an 'adapted' one and not the original.

Avoidance

Having presented an outline of the different forms of behaviour relating to dissatisfaction, we can consider each in more detail. Forms of physical avoidance, absenteeism and turnover, while they present few conceptual problems, do serve to show the complexity of relationships between indicators and concepts. There is evidence that both are negatively correlated with intrinsic job rewards (length of training and work-cycle; Baldamus 1961), job satisfaction (Palmer *et al.*, 1962) and size of organisation (Ingham, 1970a). However, it is scarcely surprising that the relationships found are not of a very high order. For example, in many of the situations where absenteeism could be expected to be high, it is also likely to be the case that financial rewards are low. If that is so, then the impact of the absenteeism in financial terms becomes greater, and it is less likely to be adopted as a form of avoidance. Similarly, with turnover an important consideration will be the existence and relative attractive-

ness of other opportunities, a factor which will vary between communities, occupations and age groups as well as over time. Both forms
of behaviour are also strongly influenced by the salience of employment for the individual. Where this is low, as with many married
women, for example, the costs involved are perceived as being far less
significant.

An important point to note is that the rewards and conditions which
foster lower absenteeism and turnover do not necessarily lead to
higher commitment to the organisation. Whether or not they do so
will depend firstly on the extent to which the rewards are seen as being
derived from, and not merely in, the organisation, and secondly on
the extent to which aspects of the work situation lead to the lower
levels of absenteeism and turnover being accompanied by compen-
satory higher levels of other forms of avoidance. In cases, for
example, where attempts are made to foster group cohesion, one
might predict a move towards a more adaptive form of behaviour, in
particular the development of informal group control over output and
so on. Direct evidence on the effect of conditions determining forms
of avoidance is hard to find, and the nearest is perhaps Sayles' (1958)
'apathetic' work groups, where turnover certainly is high and
grievance activity low (there is no mention of absenteeism). One of the
problems here, in fact, is that higher rewards and the conditions for
group action tend to be found together, especially among manual
workers, and it is difficult to separate their effects. It has, however,
been suggested (Handy, 1968) that an increase in absenteeism in the
British coal industry since 1957 could in large part be seen as
compensating for the decline in the number of strikes.

A significant feature of employing organisations in modern
industrial societies is that they provide, in principle for all their
members, mechanisms for the avoidance of particular work roles
through the assumption of other generally more rewarding roles. That
is there are, for many people, opportunities for promotion both
within the present employing organisation and by moving to others.
The importance of this is that it both sanctions a certain degree of
dissatisfaction with one's present situation, in that aspirations for
personal advancement are encouraged, and also serves to emphasise
the allocation of individuals to particular, given positions, rather than
the place of these positions within a structure of reward distribution.
So, where dissatisfaction persists it tends to lead the individual away
from placing the blame for this on the structure, and towards placing
it on himself. Or at least he may be led only to condemn details

of the processes of allocation of the system and not its basic in-equalities.

It seems very likely, therefore, that the indvidual's reliance on promotion (or rather the prospect of it) as a means of avoiding a currently dissatisfying situation reflects a pre-existing relatively high level of commitment to the organisation (and has in fact been used as an index of this – see Banks, 1963). It is unlikely that a sufficient degree of commitment can be engendered when rewards are very low, unless the opportunities for promotion are or are seen to be high, although it has been argued in the case of clerks that comparatively low rewards may go together with a high commitment and a strong valuation of advancement (Lockwood, 1958; Sykes, 1965).

However, one of the problems is that amongst those with aspirations for advancement, promotion is itself an aspect of their understanding of their situation, which thus becomes a kind of second-order reward. Since advancement is at least to some extent a competitive process in most circumstances, there will necessarily be those in whom expectations have been raised but left unsatisfied. The actual degree of mobility appears to be an important factor in deter-mining an individual's expectations, with a strong possibility that a high rate of promotions will encourage too high expectations and hence greater dissatisfaction (Merton and Kitt, 1952).

Psychological withdrawal

If there is a general problem in considering forms of adaptation, it becomes several times greater in considering those outcomes which relate to individual psychological states or attitudes rather than to behaviour, or even potential behaviour. The basis of the argument that we wish to make in this section is that one must distinguish between attitudes which directly reflect, in a fairly clear way, hostility or desire for change and those attitudes which do not necessarily overtly suggest this. Following our general argument we claim that one can identify certain attitudes as a consequence of individual avoidance of situations bringing about dissatisfaction. The difficulties of this line of argument are two-fold. Firstly there is the problem that empirically one is likely to find that the distinction made above is in many cases blurred. That is, there will usually be found a combination, with varying degrees of each, of both attitudes reflecting hostility and those reflecting avoidance. Secondly, the kind of avoidance that we are considering is in many cases difficult to distinguish from other processes. In particular a significant means of avoiding the dissatisfactions in a situation is by reducing the expectations brought to it. Exactly how this occurs raises the question of the nature of 'realistic' as against 'ideal' expectations, which is dealt with at greater length in Chapter 3. For the moment it is sufficient to point out that conceptually, and even more empirically, there are substantial problems involved in trying to separate out what are in some sense 'original' or 'basic' expectations from those that have resulted from individual avoidance by accommodation.

An indication of the significance of the distinction that is being made here can be gained from considering some of those studies which have dealt with apathy among employees. Three studies in particular: those of Sayles (1958), Scott *et al.* (1956) and Banks (1963), pointed to the existence of individuals for whom employment seems to have very low salience. To a certain extent they expressed negative or hostile attitudes towards the employing organisation, but these were never reflected in any form of behaviour designed to improve their situation. Their most important feature, however, was their apathy – their apparent generally low concern with their situation. Since these people were amongst the lowest-paid, unskilled workers, it is unlikely that their apathy reflected relative contentment with their lot. Rather, on our argument, it reflected on the one hand, experience of and perhaps conscious dislike of a situation of relative disadvantage coupled with, on the other, inability to do anything about it. Significantly, Sayles' 'apathetic' work groups are low on cohesiveness – their jobs tend to be individual operations or they are part of a long assembly line, they are unskilled and there is a high turnover of membership, while in the Scott *et al.* study the low-morale, apathetic individuals were not part of interdependent work teams, belonged to groups with unstable membership, and were on a day-wage rather than a piece-rate payment system. In both cases the basis for shared interests and group cohesion scarcely existed. The only retreat, therefore, was to attempt to divorce oneself psychologically from the situation, and to avoid involvement in and concern with it.

The apathetic workers described in these studies could also, and perhaps better, be regarded as alienated. However, it is important to remember our earlier emphasis on the distinction between this set of attitudes – apathy or alienation – and those which directly reflect conscious hostility to the organisation. Since the concept of alienation has been applied to such expressions of hostility, as well as to rather more general ideas of poor social integration (e.g. Nettler, 1957), it is necessary to make our usage clear. Although it would be unwise, dogmatic and pointless to claim that this represents the 'true' meaning of alienation, or that it exhausts its possibilities, our emphasis on a situation of disadvantage in conjunction with an inability to change that situation seems to us to relate more closely than do many other conceptions (e.g. Seeman, 1959; Blauner, 1964) to Marx's original ideas (Marx, 1961; Ollman, 1971, Mészáros, 1970).

The central point is that the proposed conceptualisation links the idea of an objectification of the social world (Berger and Luckmann, 1967) as a constraining force outside the individual, and over which he has no control, with the idea of self-estrangement – that is the treatment of the self, at work, as an object, a thing, rather than as a subject in the situation. Since this aspect constitutes only a relatively small part of our research we have not been able to pursue these ideas as thoroughly as we would wish (for a more extended treatment see Prandy, 1979). Our concern has been to try to deal with self-estrangement in the work situation, without considering broader questions of the more general consequences of this for the individual.

Adjustments of the situation by individuals

Since the employment situation is one in which individuals exchange their skills and effort for the various rewards that are available to them one course which is open to many is to adjust the amount of effort put in to the work. In a modern industrial society, particularly where the work involves a level of skill above the minimum, individuals are able to adjust not only their physical effort, but also the personal initiative that may make a substantial difference in the time taken over a task or the quality of the end result. It is simplistic and misleading to believe that the supply of effort necessary in employing organisations depends purely upon remunerative sanctions (cf. Etzioni, 1961). In the first place the efficacy of 'sanctions' is bound up with the realities of social relationships in the experiences they limit or facilitate. To separate remuneration from the relations of production and consumption, which it expresses, is to give employers a spurious independence of action. Issues of remuneration are, of course, important; but their significance is in terms of the practical experiences of individuals and the understandings they hold of these experiences. Differences in remuneration are generally accepted as necessary to the operation of the system, but in particular circumstances individuals, or groups of individuals, may believe that their relative returns are wilfully being kept down. The effectiveness of remunerative sanctions, in the absence of coercive control, depends upon a minimum acceptance that the level of return is not unfair. If the effort bargain is 'unfair', in the sense that it is understood to be unnecessarily low in terms of what the situation will afford, then a struggle between employer and employee will ensue.

In a one-sided adjustment of the effort bargain employees are in a sense adapting the situation by reducing their effort and involvement in it. Since these are important factors in determining their level of expectations, this is essentially a strategy for lowering the latter. However, it is basically a negative strategy, and could almost be regarded as avoidance rather than adaptation. In so far as individuals are reducing their effort below a level that they would be prepared to expend, then they are still not receiving the returns that they would expect from the higher level, and the relief of dissatisfaction is only partial. Furthermore, by limiting their involvement they are increasing the likelihood of their own self-estrangement.

At this point it is important to distinguish the two forms in which this individual adaptation may occur. On the one hand there are adaptations by individuals which are *standard* features of social processes. For example, young people entering employment for the first time, or people moving from one form of employment to another, may engage in fairly lengthy periods of adjustment. For the individuals the situations are to some extent novel and problematic, but they are regularly repeated in the reproduction of the system. The accommodations are thus best regarded as standard processes of a reproducing system. On the other hand circumstances which disrupt standard practices may give rise to very similar problems from the perspective of individuals. However, the processes which produced these problems and (potentially) the solutions of the problems represent to a greater or lesser extent a new state of the system.

For the most part the relationship between productivity and commitment to the organisation has been considered so clear that no demonstration of it is required. Perhaps because differences in productivity are very difficult to determine, except for those doing highly standardised work (which can usually, however, be more easily controlled), few researchers have paid much attention to this aspect. Much more attention has been given to the related phenomenon of group control of output.

Informal collective adjustments

One of the difficulties for individuals in attempting to adjust their own effort bargain is that they may well find themselves placed in competition with other individuals and thus obliged to try at least to maintain comparability in the eyes of their employer. In such situations, attempts to adjust relative rewards stand a much greater chance of success if pursued in combination with other individuals. To a certain extent, shared perceptions of fair effort and return arising from similar circumstances will ensure a degree of unanimity, but without adequate group cohesion the ability to resist fragmentation and to enforce joint understanding against employers' opposition is precarious. However, group cohesion must rest on adequate conditions for its achievement, and only on the basis of such conditions can there be successful group control of productivity. The fact that cohesion is a prerequisite of control demonstrates how facile is the assumption of a positive relationship between primary group satisfactions and commitment to the organisation. The Hawthorne studies (Roethlisberger and Dickson, 1939), which 'discovered' the importance of the primary group as an aid to higher productivity (the women of the Relay Assembly Test Room) also turned up the other aspect – what the researchers saw as the 'irrational' restriction of output (the men of the Bank Wiring Observation Room), and it is therefore surprising that such an assumption ever came to be made.

Studies in this area have suffered from the problem that our approach has tried to overcome, that of being unable to distinguish those factors which lead to a discrepancy between rewards and expectations from those which determine a particular behavioural outcome of such a discrepancy. What is perhaps the classic study in this area, that of Dalton (see Whyte, 1955), concerned itself primarily with differences in orientations that individuals import into the work situation. Thus his 'ratebusters' tended to be men of rural or middle-class background, with a strong belief in the virtues of individualism and in the pursuit of economic self-interest. This was in contrast to the 'restricters', who were far more concerned with what they saw as long-term protection through collective action. Given these different orientations, Whyte attempted to explain the conformity of individuals to the group norms. However, the research design prevented him from dealing with variations in the degree of group control of output, except in so far as this might be due to differing proportions of workers with 'ratebuster' attitudes. From a long-term point of view his work offers no explanation of the genesis of the restrictive attitudes of his working-class subjects, nor indeed of forms of collective control generally, examples of which are also found amongst non-manual employees (Blau and Scott, 1963, ch. 4). It is not clear from Dalton's study to what extent the deviance of the ratebusters might be attributable to the fact that they differed from the majority of their fellow-workers with respect to social background (cf. Rose, 1972).

The importance of social background, or better perhaps of those aspects of it which are perceived to be significant, was documented in the work of Zaleznik, Christensen and Roethlisberger (1958). Following Homans, they set out to test the hypothesis that the greater the extent of shared attributes, the greater the cohesion of the group. Homogeneity was important with respect not only to 'imported' attributes, but also to those within the work situation. Thus one would predict that similarity of work would provide a good basis for cohesion, as also, even more, would interdependence, since here a group is actually created by the formal organisation of the job and is maintained through constant interaction. Group stability and a low rate of membership turnover provide further conditions encouraging homogeneity.

Further evidence in this area comes from Lupton (1963) and from Cunnison (1966). Both studies, being based on participant observation, unfortunately dealt with only a limited situation. However, the former argued that two 'polar clusters' of factors were important in encouraging group control of production, including stability of employment, the degree of breakdown of job components and the nature of management–worker relationships, especially the extent of traditionalism. The second study emphasised the importance of the state of the product and labour markets. In times of job scarcity, competition between individuals reduced group cohesion.

As with individual adjustments, informal group activities are involved with both the maintenance and change of current arrangements in complex ways. To a large extent individuals must accommodate the practices they find in their employment circumstances, but collective action is enhanced or restricted by variations in a wide variety of social experiences, and itself can give rise to effective action for change. However, of itself a collective identity is not necessarily radical, even where it has arisen in circumstances of struggle.

Formal collective adjustments

Before going on to consider the conditions which are conducive to the development of formal collective patterns of adaptation, it is important to point out that one cannot in fact make quite such a clear-cut distinction between informal and formal. The emphasis in this section is on institutionalised machinery for managing, or attempting to bring about changes in, the work situation. In this sense the distinction is fairly straightforward, but a number of studies have shown that informal work groups are also significant in determining the use made of the formal institutions. The work of both Sayles (1958), and Scott *et al.* (1956) makes clear that those factors which encourage group cohesiveness – stability of membership, technology, job control and occupational identity – also encourage participation in, and hence benefit from, trade union activity.

Indeed, for many groups of manual workers for whom trade unions are already well established in a system of institutionalised collective bargaining, the interesting question is less that of membership or non-membership in a trade union than the extent of involvement in the union and the nature of its activities. This is probably less true of non-manual workers, which is one reason why sociologists have paid much more attention to the question of their unionisation. In all cases, however, the important point is to use meaningful indicators of union involvement.

In his overview of the available literature at the time on participation by union activists, Spinrad (1960) concluded that the major factors in encouraging participation were homogeneity of interests and communications within a group. He also pointed out that participation was associated with relatively higher job satisfaction. This finding, which is supported by several of the works referred to earlier, is a central one for our argument that organised, collective action is most likely to occur among those groups which, while they experience some dissatisfaction with their work situation, have the necessary conditions for such action. Basically, these are homogeneity of interests and good intra-group communications. Additionally, one could add the condition that the individuals involved, unlike the apathetic or alienated described above, are able to perceive their situation as one over which they have a good probability of being able to exercise some control. To a large extent such perceptions are themselves encouraged by the awareness, enhanced by communications, of interests shared with others. Equally important is the effect of successful collective action in reinforcing the perceptions. In these latter circumstances employee organisations are both standard features of employment arrangements and tokens of collective competence.

Evidence for the importance of shared interests and communications comes not only from the fact of the historical development of trade unions, the first successful examples of which were those of higher-skilled manual workers, but also, for example, from Kerr and Siegel's (1954) study of the inter-industry propensity to strike. While militancy is not an entirely satisfactory indicator of union involvement, since it depends on the reactions of employers and may reflect the failure rather than the success of union action, their general argument for the importance of community isolation probably still holds good. More direct evidence on union participation and its relationship with group cohesiveness comes from the works of Lipset, Trow and Coleman (1956), Banks (1963) and Coleman (1964). In the field of white-collar unionisation, size of the employing organisation and associated changes in administrative structure have been stressed by Lockwood (1958) and Bain (1970), and size of operating unit by Blackburn (1967). Larger organisations usually have larger units which concentrate workers together more, while the greater degree of bureaucratisation that this often entails gives them common cause in relation to universalistic rules and procedures. Lockwood also emphasises technological changes which have not only decreased the intrinsic rewards available to clerical workers, but also increased their homogeneity. He, and others, have argued further that there has been an accompanying decline in opportunities for promotion, the legitimate strategy of change, and that this is a further reason for the move towards more collective forms of action. In fact there has almost certainly been an increase in opportunities for men, but accompanied by greater importance and higher expectations of promotion, with the same outcome. The low promotion prospects are confined to the growing number of women clerks whose expectations are generally low and who tend to follow other courses of avoidance or adaptation (e.g. turnover, low involvement).

As with the other forms of adaptation we have been discussing trade unionism need not overtly reflect or imply a desire for social change.

Manual trade unions are overwhelmingly accepted by large employers as part of the process of managing the relations of production and so increasingly are non-manual unions. The ease with which most employers have accepted, or even welcomed, the closed shop illustrates the value to employers, especially those with highly bureaucratised systems, of comprehensive and comprehensible representation. Nonetheless growing unionisation usually arises out of work situations that are in some way unsatisfactory, and represents a desire for change. Even where high levels of unionism are well established both sides understand that they are in competition for resources and that the stable relationships between them can be disrupted, bringing a struggle for a new balance of costs and benefits. As the representatives of one side of divided interests, trade unions are always potentially instruments of change. Of course, change of this sort is primarily concerned with distribution and redistribution. Whether trade unionism contributes to more fundamental change is a much wider issue. Perhaps in the short run it does not, but we shall argue in our companion volume that in the long term it does. This is not because of its contribution to class consciousness and revolutionary change, as usually understood, but because it is itself an aspect of change. Inherent in it is a denial of the market principle and the development of collective understandings, both of which are part of a wider process which undermines capitalism theoretically and practically. In this volume we shall be concerned only with the preconditions and determinants of individual dispositions towards collective representation, placing these in the context of the reproduction of a system of inequality.

2 Research Strategy

The research on which we report here is based on a survey of non-manual employees in a wide range of occupations, from supervisors and clerks to senior managers, and an extensive, systematic analysis of an unusually comprehensive range of data. A general principle that guided us in the planning was the desirability of constantly relating theoretical ideas to empirical research procedures. Consequently we tried both to elaborate the theory as precisely as possible, and also to collect the data in such a way as to maximise our chances of providing an adequate test of the theory. We were well aware that an over-precise theory might well violate the complexity of the situation, and also that the use of particular techniques often requires assumptions that the data do not strictly meet. On the other hand, a complex verbal theory is more difficult to test, while certain techniques make possible not only a more adequate test, but also a more precise analysis of the relationships involved. Beyond the simplest case of the isolated consideration of single hypotheses it becomes necessary to use techniques of multivariate analysis, many of which require data which have been satisfactorily measured at the interval level. Our use of several kinds of multivariate analysis and our attempts to improve methods of measurement are left for description in later sections. First we shall describe in some detail the procedures that were used in collecting data, and the nature of the population from which they were collected.

COLLECTION OF THE DATA

The population which was of interest to us was, in general terms, that of male, non-manual employees. Our interest in non-manual or white-collar workers stems in part at least from the previous work of two of the present authors (Blackburn, 1967; Prandy, 1965a). Since one of our major concerns was with the question of union commitment, non-manual workers, for many of whom this is at present a real issue of

26

choice, constitute the best group for study. Also they provide rather more homogeneity than would be the case if manual workers were also included. Clearly this implies a limitation on the empirical testing of our theoretical scheme, but it is a necessary compromise if too much complexity is to be avoided.

For similar reasons we chose to restrict our study to men. To have included women in the analysis would have meant the introduction of additional variables. We would have needed to incorporate, for example, the different significance that work has for them compared to men. In addition it would have affected the balance of the population studied by introducing a large number of people doing very much the same kind of work. This problem, that the sex difference is also highly correlated with particular occupational experiences, would have raised serious difficulties in analysis. On the other hand the tendency for men and women to be employed in different jobs does make a single-sex study meaningful.

An original restriction of our study to employees in private industry, which in fact we were later able to relax, was also due to the need to concentrate in the first instance on those groups where unionisation was most problematic. A similar compromise in relation to economy of effort and resources was that we decided to study only firms within a radius of approximately 60 miles from Cambridge, and only those with a total number of employees, within the establishment, exceeding 500.

The 60-mile radius limitation is not as serious as it may at first sight appear. It covers virtually the whole of East Anglia together with, moving clockwise, London, Bedfordshire and Hertfordshire, and part of the East Midlands (Northampton, Wellingborough, etc.). With one exception, an insurance company head office in the City, we restricted our choice in London to the northern area beyond the North Circular Road, taking in, for example, both the relatively older areas to the east, such as Dagenham and Barking, and the new, 'lighter' industrial areas to the north-west. It thus includes areas of recent growth and relatively high mobility, and those of old-established, though small-scale, industrial firms.

We decided to deal with establishments rather than with companies because we thought that, all things considered, these constituted more meaningful productive units. Thus there was more likely to be a degree of homogeneity of administrative policy or representation within an establishment, and we could consistently apply those measures relating to the overall context of employment to such units.

The decision to restrict the study to those of over 500 employees was also less limiting than it might seem, and was again related to the particular focus of the study on union membership. While it is true that industrial establishments of less than 500 employees account for a substantial proportion of employment, they tend to have a very small number of male, non-manual employees. It seemed unlikely that there would be many union members to be found in such establishments, and although we were as much interested in non-members as in members, to have included any number of small firms would have risked swamping the latter with the former. Furthermore, establishments below this size are likely to be different in a number of respects from the larger ones, and we again felt the need to restrict the range of some variables in order to consider others more fruitfully.

Another important practical consideration dictating this choice of larger establishments only was the difficulty and effort involved in making arrangements with firms for carrying out interviews. The interviewing had to be organised through the firm since it provided the only basis on which a sampling frame could be constructed. The trade unions themselves might have offered an alternative basis, but this would not have helped secure a sample of non-members, neither would it have allowed us to cover very adequately the possible means of representation other than trade unions. Furthermore the approach through the firm, or establishment, also enabled us to collect data on the latter which would not have been available had we tried to sample individuals directly.

As we noted above, we were able to extend our coverage of establishments beyond private manufacturing industry. This brought in a variety of organisations where the staff are predominantly non-manual, so that the size restriction was no longer necessary. However, it will be clearer if, to start with, we limit our description to the original sample.

The selection of the respondents, the individuals who form the basic units of analysis, was carried out in two stages. First came the selection of establishments and then the selection of individuals within each establishment. In selecting establishments we were guided by the general principle of choosing one's objects of study according to their theoretical relevance, rather than by some criterion based on their frequency in a population. That is, we were concerned with 'scope sampling' (Willer, 1967) rather than random sampling. The importance of this distinction lies in the fact that most sampling procedures are concerned with adequately representing, and generalising back to, a population. Theories, on the other hand, are not concerned with specific populations but with general hypotheses, though they may of course hold only under specific conditions to be found in a particular population. Given the variables on which we chose to concentrate, we wished to select cases in such a way that we would secure an adequate range of values of each variable. Of course this is not to deny the importance of randomness in selection as a means of overcoming problems of spurious relationships that might be introduced by the observer, but it is to emphasise that identification of parameters in and generalising to a population is not the primary concern in theoretical analysis. Whether, indeed, establishments of over 500 employees within a 60-mile radius of Cambridge constitute a meaningful population in any sense is very questionable anyway.

In many cases the optimum solution is to stratify one's population on important variables, to secure an adequate range for purposes of analysis, and to sample independently within the strata. However, when the total population is comparatively small and the number of variables and/or strata within variables is large, this procedure is rather difficult, since the individual 'sub-populations' can become very small or even non-existent. In this situation, which is the one that we faced, a form of quota sampling, in which one aims for a particular distribution on a number of variables, has to be resorted to.

Before going on to consider the nature of the sampling problem it is necessary to describe the way in which the sampling frame was constructed. Here we relied primarily on a trade publication, *Kompass* (1968), one volume of which gives a listing of manufacturers by county, and by towns within counties. In the majority of cases information on the number of employees is included. The directory is not always consistent in dealing with companies which have more than one establishment; sometimes each is given separately, but not always. However, very often the listing of the head office of the company would also give the location of the manufacturing units. So, with only a small amount of supplementary use of other directories or of personal knowledge, we were satisfied that we constructed an adequate sampling frame of establishments of the size in which we were interested.

What, then, were the considerations that we bore in mind in selecting firms? The major ones were the size of the establishment, the industry, and the geographical location. For the first we used the three categories of small (under 1000 employees), medium (1000 to 1999 employees) and large (2000 employees and over). For the last, we

TABLE 2.1 *Establishments in survey area (sample numbers in parentheses): location and industry by size*

	Small	Medium	Large	Total
Location				
Metropolitan				
GLC	61 (1)	33 (4)	29	123 (5)
Outer London	79 (1)	44 (4)	32 (1)	155 (6)
East Midlands	22 (1)	14 (2)	8 (1)	44 (4)
East Anglia	61 (2)	25 (1)	24 (1)	110 (4)
SIC				
3 Food and drink	19 (1)	10	8	37 (1)
4 Chemicals	24 (1)	13 (3)	6	43 (4)
5 Metal manufacture	7	4	2	13
6 Engineering and electrical	76 (2)	42 (6)	47 (1)	165 (9)
8 Vehicles	14	8	13 (1)	35 (1)
9 Metal goods	7	5	3	15
10 Textiles	3	1	1	5
11 Leather goods	–	1	–	1
12 Clothing and footwear	15 (1)	8	4 (1)	27 (2)
13 Bricks, pottery, glass	5	5 (1)	1	11 (1)
14 Furniture	9	4	–	13
15 Paper and printing	15	4	3	22
16 Other manufacturing	12	5 (1)	–	19 (1)
Total	206 (5)	110 (11)	90 (3)	406 (19)

divided the whole area into three parts – Metropolitan, East Midlands and East Anglia. The Standard Industrial Classification (SIC) was used for industry. Table 2.1 shows the actual numbers of establishments within our area, broken down by size and geographical location, and then by size and industry. The population of establishments in this area shows a preponderance of small establishments, of establishments in engineering and of establishments in the Metropolitan, particularly the Outer London, region. While the actual availability of establishments is clearly a constraint, our intention was to try to choose them so as to achieve an even balance between our categories of size, industry and location. The table also shows the degree of our success in this regard. While we were fairly successful in respect of geographical location we were rather less so in the case of the other two criteria. To a certain extent this was because, as we began to select replacements for establishments which did not wish to co-operate (a point which will be taken up shortly), our criteria for selection became contradictory. So, although we were able to achieve proper representation of medium-sized as against small establishments, we were unable to do so for the large ones. Since the engineering industry accounts for 54 per cent of the latter, it would have been difficult to achieve adequate representation of large firms without thereby over-representing those in engineering.

Size and geographical location have previously been discussed as variables that we wished to control, but type of industry has not, and it is important to make clear what were our intentions here. Stratifying the sample by industrial classification was not designed primarily to secure representation, nor even to achieve over- or under-representation. Rather, we regarded industrial category as a crude, summary indicator of a variety of other variables, and we selected four of these, on which published data were available, as particularly significant for our purposes. Of course there was no guarantee that a particular establishment would necessarily be typical for that industry, but we believed that some knowledge was better than none. The four variables selected were: (1) proportion of male non-manual employees; (2) index of production – i.e. an indication of the rate of growth or decline of an industry; (3) value of output per employee; and (4) average earnings of non-manual employees. Each industry was categorised as high, medium or low in each case on the basis of its rank-order position. We then tried to ensure that firms were selected from the various industrial categories in such a way that we could expect to have at least one establishment in each of the three categories for the four variables. We also had in mind that the structure of staff representation is to a fair extent related to industry, so that our selection procedure might be expected to give variation in this respect, although unfortunately we were not able to include this factor explicitly. In Table 2.2 we show the distribution of these categories by industry (for those industries with a reasonable number of establishments in our area) and also the distribution of establishments finally selected.

If the selection of establishments were to be regarded as a normal sampling process then it would have to be admitted that the final set of establishments chosen are rather suspect. It is no easy matter to interest the management of a firm in allowing one to disrupt their normal routine by interviewing a substantial number of their non-manual staff. Most firms, which were first approached by letter, were unwilling even to discuss the possibility of the research, and we were

TABLE 2.2 *Major industries characterised by level on four indicators*

	Male non-manual employees	Index of production	Output per employee	Non-manual earnings
SIC				
3 Food and drink	M	L	H	H
4 Chemicals	H	H	H	H
6 Engineering and electrical	H	H	M	L
8 Vehicles	H	M	M	H
9 Metal goods	M	L	M	M
12 Clothing and footwear	L	M	L	M
13 Bricks, pottery, glass	M	H	M	L
15 Paper and printing	H	M	H	H
16 Other manufacturing	M	H	M	M
Sample establishments				
High	14	15	5	6
Medium	3	3	12	3
Low	2	1	2	10

H = high level; M = medium level; L = low level.

unable to persuade all of those who agreed to see us about it. On the other hand almost all those who did agree to assist us showed a positive interest in the research and were very co-operative. A full account of firms approached and the reasons given for refusal is set out in Table 2.3. It can be seen from this that co-operation was most difficult to obtain from the food and drinks industry (SIC 3) and from large establishments, particularly in engineering (SIC 6). The most common reason given for not wishing to co-operate was the time and disruption involved, while a number of firms pointed out that they were, or had recently been, involved in research projects. It is of course very difficult to assess how far the process of self-selection which is occurring here has resulted in a highly unusual set of establishments. It is likely that we missed those companies which were involved in reorganisation consequent upon takeovers and mergers (GEC–AEI establishments constitute a substantial proportion of the larger ones in engineering in our area), and perhaps also some where management had problems, temporary or otherwise, with non-manual representation. However, we would not regard the establishments chosen as particularly unusual, and in any case for most purposes the

TABLE 2.3 Establishments approached and reasons for refusal, by industry and size

SIC*	Size	Total approached	No answer	Refused immediately					Refused after discussion				
				No reason	'Time'	'Representation'	Other research	Reorganisation	No reason	'Time'	'Representation'	Other research	Reorganisation
3	S	3	—	—	1	—	—	—	—	—	—	—	—
	M	5	1	2	1	—	—	—	—	—	—	1	—
	L	5	—	—	1	—	—	1	2	—	—	—	—
4	S	6	2	2	2	—	1	1	—	—	—	1	—
	M	4	—	—	—	—	—	1	—	1	—	1	—
	L	4	—	1	1	—	1	1	1	—	—	—	—
6	S	5	—	1	—	1	—	—	1	—	—	—	—
	M	13	—	2	7	1	5	2	1	2	1	—	—
	L	22	—	—	2	1	—	3	1	1	—	—	1
8	S	3	—	—	—	—	—	—	1	—	—	—	—
	L	3	—	1	—	—	1	1	—	1	—	—	1
9	M	1	2	1	—	—	—	—	—	—	—	—	—
12	S	3	1	—	—	—	1	1	—	—	—	—	—
	M	1	1	—	—	—	—	—	—	—	—	—	—
	L	2	—	—	—	—	1	1	—	—	—	—	—
13	M	1	—	1	—	—	—	—	—	—	—	—	—
15	S	2	—	1	—	1	—	—	—	1	—	—	—
	L	1	—	1	—	—	—	—	—	—	—	—	—
16	M	2	2	1	1	—	1	—	1	1	—	2	2
Total	S	22	2	4	5	1	1	2	1	1	—	2	—
	M	27	2	3	1	1	—	2	1	3	1	2	—
	L	38	—	5	9	1	7	6	3	—	—	—	2
Total		87	4	12	15	3	8	10	5	4	1	4	2

* See Table 2.2 FOR SIC groupings.

influence of bias would have to be indirect, since most of our analysis relates to variables measured on individuals. While the selection of firms was less satisfactory than we would have wished, and needs to be taken into account, it would be a mistake to exaggerate its importance for the analysis presented in this study.

The selection of individuals within each establishment was fortunately a much more straightforward procedure. We defined as non-manual those who came into the occupational categories of supervisor, clerk, draughtsman, technician, professional or manager. In almost all the firms this corresponded to their 'staff' or 'weekly- or monthly-paid' employees. Since, however, the latter group included security men in most cases, we decided also to sample these. As far as possible we tried to restrict respondents to those aged 21 or over. From lists of the names of male non-manual employees who normally worked full-time within the establishment, we selected respondents on a simple random sample basis using tables of random numbers. The only complication we introduced relates to the sampling fraction, and we used a formula to calculate this, such that the proportion chosen for interview declined as the total available for interview increased. In effect, the sample size increases logarithmically rather than linearly with the size of the population. The rationale for this can be related to our reason for choosing to interview a substantial number of people in a small number of establishments, rather than a few people in many establishments. Very likely, the latter procedure would have ensured a higher rate of co-operation from firms, but our decision to adopt the former method was made so that we could make some attempt to deal with contextual effects (Lazarsfeld and Menzel, 1961; Lazarsfeld, 1959). That is, in addition to collecting data on each individual, we wished to collect data on the various collectivities within which he might be located. In part, for all respondents, this could be obtained from management, where it related to the establishment, and from local union officials, where this was appropriate. However, not all of the data that we wanted were of this kind; that is, they did not relate to a formal collectivity. We also wanted data that could only be secured by aggregating the responses of individuals. This meant that we had to have enough respondents within each enterprise, and preferably also within each broad occupational grouping within the enterprise, to provide reasonably significant data. In the case of small establishments, or rather establishments with a smaller number of male non-manual employees, this required us to use a fairly large sampling fraction, whereas in establishments with a greater number that sampling fraction could be reduced.

The undoubted convenience of this procedure is to some extent, though not to our mind sufficiently, offset by a potential problem that it creates. It is possible in some cases that relationships in which we are interested may be different in establishments of differing size – that is, there may be an interaction effect between size and the relationship between two other variables. Our weighting procedures, both in selecting establishments and in selecting the proportion of respondents within each establishment, will in this situation mean that the relationship found within our sample of respondents will not be the same as that in the population. Again, however, the point must be made that our concern is not with a population of respondents but with a structure of relationships, and if interaction effects of this kind are present then the best way to deal with them is to take them explicitly into account. In fact, as far as the material presented in this volume is concerned we were not able to detect any such effects.

The proportion selected for interview in each firm ranged from about 46 per cent in an establishment with 35 male non-manual employees to 12 per cent in one with nearly 1900. In all, 1597 respondents were approached in manufacturing firms, of whom 1288 (81 per cent) were interviewed. Since we carried out the interviewing within each establishment within a period of, on average, about a week, part of the non-response is due to absence through sickness, holiday or business elsewhere. The response rate varied between establishments, from 67 per cent to 94 per cent, with an average, disregarding size, of 77 per cent. Overall, the response rate may be regarded as satisfactory.

It became apparent during the fieldwork in manufacturing firms that it would be possible, as we had hoped, to extend our coverage to establishments of other kinds. Consequently we added to the 19 in manufacturing, two insurance company head offices, the head office of a public utility, four local government establishments, two national government establishments, two research laboratories, and the head office of a building contracting company. In terms of the numbers of non-manual workers these covered a similar range to that of the manufacturing sample. The geographical spread was a little different from that of the manufacturing establishments (Table 2.1) in that a majority of these were in East Anglia – seven compared with two in the East Midlands, two in Outer London and one in the GLC area. Very little difficulty was experienced in obtaining co-operation in any of these cases. The method of selecting respondents was the same, except that in all cases smaller sampling fractions were used than in manufacturing, since we expected to find greater occupational homogeneity. The total number of new respondents sampled was 757, of whom 636 (84 per cent) were interviewed. Thus the total number interviewed was 1924. Subsequently, however, six of these were dropped from the sample because of the relatively large number of unanswered questions.

All respondents were asked to complete a checklist before attending the interview. The interview itself usually lasted from 30 to 40 minutes. Both the checklist and the interview schedule are reproduced in Appendix I.

MEASUREMENT

Inadequate measurement probably represents the greatest problem in the application of multivariate techniques to sociological analysis. In this section we shall discuss our general approach to this problem and the methods that were used to try to minimise it. For the most part discussion of actual measures, that is the indicators used as operational representations of theoretical concepts, is left until each is introduced in the context of the analysis and theoretical argument. The present concern is with the general principles of measurement which we tried to apply wherever possible in each particular instance.

In practice, of course, one cannot deal separately with the theoretical problem of operationalisation and the technical problem of method of measurement. A decision often has to be taken either to use an indicator which is not completely adequate from a theoretical point of view, but which is easily and cheaply measured, or to try to develop another which might be far more adequate, but would be much more difficult to measure. A number of our measures represent the choice of the first of these alternatives – for example, in using such indicators as age, number of years of education, length of service in the company, number of times a person moved house, size of community of upbringing, total time spent interacting with other persons at work, or number of people working in the same room, to represent a variety of aspects of life experience. These indicators present few problems with regard to measurement, but their theoretical status is less clear.

In some cases one has to accept both doubt about theoretical adequacy and measurement at less than interval level. A number of the measures that we use in relation to individual perceptions are attempts to present respondents with a sufficient number of ordered response categories for us to be able to treat them as if there were unit intervals between them. This is the thinking behind the use of continuous lines, with only broad segments verbally labelled (see, for example, any of the satisfaction items in Chapter 5). In fact, there was a fairly strong tendency for responses to cluster around the verbal labels, and it is not clear whether the more successful strategy would be to reduce or to increase the number of these (although pilot results from other research suggest that the latter is to be preferred). The major problem remains, however, whether individuals have any very clear conception of, say, their satisfaction, and even more whether they are able to express it in anything other than crude categories, the 'true' meaning of which may vary from one person to another.

The position is more satisfactory when one is able to use a number of indicators to develop a measure of a theoretical concept, since here it is possible to use various techniques which give both an indication of the extent to which the indicators are measuring a single concept, and also perhaps information on the relation of the indicators to each other. In two cases we have made use of preferential choice data (Coombs, 1964), which can be analysed using the basic logic of unfolding theory. In practice, however, a numerical rather than an analytical method is required, using one of the variety of programs available to deal with multidimensional scaling. In the case of two scales referred to we used MINISSA or MINILSA (Roskam, 1969) as appropriate. Both scales, one of enterprise unionateness and the other of stratification arrangements, have been described in greater detail elsewhere (Prandy, Stewart and Blackburn, 1974; Stewart, Prandy and Blackburn, 1980) and it is unnecessary here to go into great detail on the techniques involved. The first of them is discussed a little more fully in Chapter 6, but in view of the widespread use that we make of the second it is useful to give a brief description here.

As part of the interview we asked respondents to think of people with whom they were friendly outside work, and to tell us the occupations of (up to) four of them. Our respondents and their friends were all coded in accordance with the Office of Population Censuses and Surveys' *Classification of Occupations*, 1970. Then, for all those in each occupational category we were able to set out the distribution of all of their friends across the same set of categories. These distributions could be compared with one another to create a set of pair-wise dissimilarity coefficients. Briefly, the more similar are a pair of distributions, the lower is the value of the coefficient, and the more unlike they are the higher it is. The range is from nought to one. The coefficients of dissimilarity can be regarded as a measure of the distance between two occupational categories, and the problem then becomes one of ascertaining whether the occupations can be positioned in a space of reasonably low dimensionality, in such a way that the various estimates of distance can be made consistent with one another. If this is possible, then one of the dimensions in the space, and preferably a large one, may represent the hypothesised scale of stratification, though, as with any measure, the adequacy of the representations can only be judged against existing ideas and knowledge.

In the present instance, as is explained in Stewart, Prandy and Blackburn (1980), this method not only produces a more satisfactory scale than any other, but does so on the basis of a more convincing set of theoretical assumptions. For simplicity we shall refer to this by the conventional term as an 'occupational status' scale, but this label should not be taken too literally. We should emphasise that our measure, unlike most others in this area, does not attempt to tap perceptions of status ordering or of the relative standing of occupations. Instead, it reflects the hierarchical ordering of overall lifestyles and social interactions. An abridged version of the scale is reproduced as Table 2.4.

As we believe this example shows well, the methods available for the analysis of preferential choice data provide one of the most useful and powerful tools of measurement available to sociology. A minimum of assumptions are imposed on the data but a maximum of information, both about the stimuli and the respondents, is extracted.

The remaining set of measurement problems to be considered are all

TABLE 2.4   *Abridged Cambridge scale*

Range of scores	Typical occupational groups
0–48	Unskilled manual workers*
55–70	Skilled manual workers*
75–90	Engineering assistants and inspectors, low-level technicians
105	Clerks
114	Sales assistants
125	Supervisory clerks, office managers
135–140	Draughtsmen, laboratory technicians
175–180	Technicians*
190–200	Accountants, social workers
205–250	Managers
250–300	Professionals

* These categories include the supervisors of such occupations

concerned with combining a number of indicators to form a single scale. In cases of this kind there are two basic assumptions that one may make, and two different measurement models associated with them. The first position is that the items to be combined each represent a point on the underlying continuum that one is attempting to measure. Such an assumption is the basis for Guttman's scalogram analysis, and the commonest procedure is to treat each item as a dichotomy, which gives a set of 'pass'/'fail' responses. It is also common for items which originally have more than one response category to be dichotomised, sometimes at that point which gives the best coefficient of reproducibility. Coombs (1964; see also Schooler, 1968) rightly criticises this procedure, and also points to a more satisfactory one, which he calls disorderly interlocking. This consists essentially of reducing the n categories to $n-1$ dichotomous items. While this procedure is more sensitive to unreliability, it does enable all the information contained in the data to be used. Because of the built-in perfect scaleability of the set of dichotomies obtained from each of the original items, care is needed in the calculation of the coefficient of reproducibility. In our case we considered Green's Rep_B (Green, 1956) to be most appropriate, since it is more demanding than Guttman's original coefficient. Also it takes account of pattern inversions up to three columns apart, rather than simply those which occur between adjacent columns. It can be easily modified by ignoring pairs of columns which come from the same original item, and which are therefore necessarily perfectly scaleable. Significance tests are also available (Goodman, 1959).

Unfortunately our experience of using the modified Guttman procedure was that it was possible to obtain very high coefficients of reproducibility, with a high level of significance, whilst finding only a minority of perfect scale patterns. Thus, while the scalogram procedure is a very good means of demonstrating the scaleability of a set of items, it may well leave unsolved the problem of allocating a score to each individual respondent. The simplest solution of this problem is straightforwardly to add the scores on each of the original items. This has the advantage of giving the same result in the case of the perfect scale patterns, assuming that the scoring is on the basis of the number of positive responses. For non-perfect scale patterns this method is probably as good as any other, at least given its simplicity, since it results in a score approximately mid-way between an upper estimate of scale position, the last positive response, and a lower estimate, one before the first negative response.

However, to adopt this procedure is also to bring into question the basic assumption upon which Guttman scaling is based. If the items represent points at different intervals on an underlying continuum, then it is inappropriate to treat them as equivalent. An alternative measurement model is based on the quite different assumption that each of the items is an indicator of an underlying attribute, but that the relationship is a probabilistic one. Latent structure analysis (Lazarsfeld and Henry, 1968) provides a possible reconciliation of these two approaches, but unfortunately is poorly developed from a practical point of view. However, factor analysis is, with certain assumptions, an appropriate technique to use with such a measurement model, and we therefore chose to supplement the scalogram analysis with it. The particular method used was that of principal factors (Harman, 1967), with the communalities estimated by an iterative refactoring procedure. At each stage the values given by the factor loadings on the 'significant' factors were used as estimates of communality, where the number of significant factors is equal to the number of principal components of the correlation matrix for which the associated eigenvalues are greater than one. Such analysis can be routinely carried out on the SPSS package (Nie *et al.*, 1975).

The results of the factor analysis were used partly as a check on the homogeneity of the items, but mainly to provide weightings that could be applied to the individual item scores before adding them. The weightings are such as to maximise the correlation between the constructed and the underlying factor. Again this procedure is routine in SPSS, which also allows for estimation using the mean in cases where data are missing on any of the items. The results of factor analysis were not used in those cases where only two items were combined or where there was strong evidence of items being ordered in the manner of a Guttman scale. The latter was particularly the case with our measure of society unionateness, where the correlation matrix showed clear evidence of a simplex structure (Guttman, 1954). The importance of this is discussed more fully in Prandy, Stewart and Blackburn (1974).

ANALYSIS

The principles of path analysis, which is used extensively in this report, are well known and do not need to be elaborated here (for an introduction, see Land, 1969; Heise, 1969; Blalock, 1971). Our own view is that in the present state of theoretical development, and with the generally attainable level of measurement of many important variables, it is more profitable to concentrate on path analysis, where standardised variables are used, than on regression analysis using unstandardised variables. The former has the advantage that it can also be used to extend Blalock's (1964) concern with the testing of causal models, as well as to estimate the strength of causal relationships. Of course, at base these two are essentially the same thing, and the difference is primarily one of emphasis. However, it does mean, for example, that although path coefficients are given in all cases we do not, nor do we expect our readers to, attribute any special significance to anything other than the general order of magnitude of such coefficients. Birnbaum (1977) has demonstrated that the usual claim that '*the squared path coefficient* measures the proportion of the variance of the dependent variable for which the determining variable is *directly* responsible' (Land, 1969, 10) is valid only on the highly implausible assumption that all units of analysis – in our case people – react identically to a change in any of the variables. The important point is that even with a degree of scepticism, the gain in theoretical understanding and knowledge over more straightforward methods is considerable.

One of the problems with regression analysis in any form is how to deal with variables which have not been measured at the interval level. Where a reasonable number of ordered categories are available for a particular variable there is probably more to be gained from treating it as an equal-interval scale than is lost through the strict falsity of the assumption (cf. Labovitz, 1970).

In other cases, such as for example when the measurement is whether the respondent's father was himself ever a member of a trade union, the variable is no more than a dichotomy anyway. The solution in the normal regression approach is to treat the dichotomies as dummy variables, that is to give each a score of 0 or 1. The coefficients then have a fairly simple interpretation as the amount by which the intercept term changes when that factor is present, or put another way the addition to the dependent variable made by a, which is also the, unit increase in the factor. Unfortunately neither interpretation makes intuitive sense when the dichotomy is reduced to a standardised form, since there is then no intercept term, nor is there a unit increase. Instead, the values of 0 and 1 will be transformed to values which depend on the proportion of those possessing the particular property.

One possible solution to the problem that we considered was to use a biserial correlation coefficient (Lord, 1963). This would appear to be suitable in those cases where the dichotomy is in fact a crude attempt at measuring an underlying continuous variable, but most of our uses did not come into that category. Instead, we decided to use the dichotomies as if carrying out normal standardised regression and to draw attention to the difficulty of interpretation. In practice, where the main concern is in comparing the size of different coefficients, the difficulty is not at all serious.

An important aspect of path analysis is its ability to separate out direct and indirect effects, and in general to uncover 'spurious' correlations. However, it must be remembered that any particular causal model of a set of relationships is dependent upon the variables that have been included in the model. That is, one must always assume that, for the present purposes, certain relationships genuinely exist, and cannot be explained as 'spurious' because of the operation of some unknown factor.

The first point to note, then, is that any set of results must always be taken as provisional and conditional (this is, in fact, a general truth which only has to be more explicitly acknowledged in using path analysis). Whilst there is no ultimate solution to this 'problem', it is of course one of the purposes of scientific inquiry to explore beyond given sets of relationships, particularly in the light of theoretical concerns. The second point to note, therefore, is that it is highly desirable to attempt to include a partial sub-set of relationships within a larger set. In the light of these considerations we have generally chosen to start with relationships between a limited number of variables, where the results and the theoretical discussion are comparatively easy to absorb, before introducing a larger and more complete model. This approach also has the advantage that it enables the reader to exercise his own judgement rather more concerning the adequacy of our causal schemes.

3 Social Background, Rewards and Perceptions

In the first chapter we set out our arguments for approaching social stratification in general, and employee involvement in particular, through a consideration of the structure of the distribution of rewards, individual reactions to that distribution, and the strategies that are pursued in attempting to change it. Associated with that structure are normative and cognitive elements, according to which those who possess certain criteria, such as educational qualifications, are believed to merit greater rewards, both because they possess the criteria and because possession of them is associated with the attainment of more highly rewarded positions. The cognitive aspects underpin the normative, providing a rationale for the belief in the necessity of the differential allocation of rewards. While these aspects are not, in themselves, a direct concern of this study, they are involved in the individual's perceptions of his position and in his expectations. These perceptions and expectations can only be understood in the context of his present situation and past experience, which is where we must begin. We shall leave an examination of expectations to the next chapter, but perceptions are not readily separable from the actual rewards and will be considered here. First, however, we must give our attention both to the actual structure of the distribution of rewards within our sample, and to the processes by which the individuals came to occupy the positions that they do. That is, we want to consider the ways in which various factors in the individual's background led to a particular location, and to the rewards associated with it.

Such processes are interesting in their own right, and are a critical part of the stratification system, but a consideration of them is also necessary when we are dealing with the individual's reaction to his present location. For the individual this last is part of a process, and his reaction to it is likely to be determined not solely by his current experiences, but by the way in which these fit into his total life history. Not only will the individual assess his present position in the light of what has gone before, and what he anticipates will follow, but we would expect his early socialisation and his previous experiences to have a significant effect on his cognitions of the reward distribution structure and on his evaluations of it.

We have included amongst background variables those which either are quite clearly located in a previous stage of the individual's life or are part of his social experience outside the sphere of work and employment. Thus in addition to those factors, such as the respondent's father's occupational status or his own educational experience, which are clearly and temporally in the 'background', there are also factors related to work, but which are in the past – the respondent's first job, for example – and those which are in the present, but not directly a part of his work experience – such as the occupational status of his friends. Conversely, what we regard as factors relating to location are those which relate to the respondent's present employment situation, and to the rewards that he derives from it.

The first part of this chapter, then, deals with the interrelationships amongst background variables, or at least those which were included because we anticipated that they would be significant in determining the attainment of a position and its associated rewards, the expectations regarding such rewards, or the reactions to their distribution. It then proceeds to a consideration of the role played by background factors in the attainment of a location and its associated rewards. Then, in the second half of this chapter, we shall look at the individual's perceptions of the rewards available to him at work, and these again we shall consider in relation to his background and social location.

SOCIAL BACKGROUND

What we are treating as social background spans an individual's lifetime, so it is not sufficient to look in a static manner at the effects of various background factors on the present situation. We must recognise that these factors are part of a process where some aspects of social background are influenced by others. This means that while all background variables may have a direct effect on present position or perceptions, most will also have indirect effects through one or more of the others. Thus our first step must be to explain the present pattern of background factors. In this section we shall present a model of the process linking social background to educational experience and attainment of various kinds, and link these to geographical mobility.

There are four aspects of the individual's social background that we take as basic. The two most important of these are age and father's occupational status. The importance of age, which includes period lived through and life cycle stage, hardly needs stressing, and there is little point in examining it separately. We shall consider it presently in conjunction with the other factors. The occupational status of the father has to stand as surrogate for a whole complex of factors relating to the respondent's early socialisation and to his origins within the social system. Moreover, because of problems of recall and of analysis, we felt obliged, as do most other researchers, to ask for the father's occupation at just one point in time, so ignoring the dynamic aspects of structural location. The time chosen was when the respondent left school. As with all the other cases involving occupation, we used our own scale to give a score of occupational level. It will be recalled (see Chapter 2) that though we usually refer to this as an occupational status score, it is not designed to measure the prestige of occupations but basic similarities of lifestyles. In addition to this 'fine' measure of occupational status, we also utilised a simple manual/non-manual distinction based on the OPCS categories with the exception that all supervisors were treated as non-manual.

The mean occupational status of the fathers of the men in our sample is 100, that is about the level of clerks on our scale. The figure for those in public employment is higher (117) than for those in the private sector (98), but both are at the lower end of the occupations included in our sample of non-manual workers, and well below the mean score of the respondents themselves, which is 152. This suggests that there has been considerable intergenerational 'mobility', although it is necessary to exercise caution in coming to such a conclusion. It ignores the fact that respondents' fathers were themselves still involved in a process of occupational change and thus potentially mobile. This point is less telling in so far as the average age of fathers of sons leaving schooling would be close to the mean age for our sample, that is 40 years, though it would show less dispersal. Thus a father would have been at a stage in his 'career' similar to that of the 'average' son we have interviewed.

Since our sample is entirely non-manual it is to be expected, given any degree of openness, that there would be some upward mobility from the families of manual workers. In fact 54 per cent of respondents had fathers who were manual workers, a strikingly high proportion. It is probable that intergenerational differences are largely due to structural changes, since in the relevant period these changes have been substantial, particularly in the expansion of some white-collar areas and a corresponding contraction of manual employment (cf. Goldthorpe, 1980). How far such changes may usefully be regarded as mobility or are experienced as such by individuals is problematic.

The third variable we take as given is size of community of origin. The majority of our respondents (53 per cent) were brought up in large communities (populations of over 100 000), a further 25 per cent in medium (over 5000), and 14 and 7 per cent in rural and small communities respectively. Finally, several of our sample are foreign-born. The proportion is only 2½ per cent; so small that the inclusion of this variable is not usually justified. However, it does appear that foreign-born respondents tend to have had higher-status fathers and to have been brought up in larger communities.

We would expect that educational variables would be particularly significant for the issues with which this study is concerned. We collected information on the type of school attended, the age at which the respondent left school (rescored as the number of years spent at school beyond the legal minimum at the time), his further education experience, and any qualifications he obtained. The type of school attended was reduced to a dichotomy of grammar, public and other private-sector schools, and the remainder; that is the most selective (on the grounds of ability – including the ability to pay) against the (relatively) non-selective. Since this largely represents also a status distinction in schooling, we have treated attendance at a selective school as the positive response. In fact, only a minority of our respondents (45 per cent) attended such a school. It is not surprising, therefore, that over the total sample 36 per cent left school at the minimum age and that the remainder spent an average of only 2.1 years beyond the legal minimum (allowing for the respondent's age) at school. Eighty-two per cent had no further period of full-time education, and the remainder averaged 2.9 years. However, as we would expect, in terms of both the type of school attended and the time spent in full-time education, our white-collar sample is much better educated than the general population.

Significantly, part-time further education has been more widely experienced. Twenty-seven per cent had some day-time further education experience, with an average of 3.7 years, and 53 per cent some evening education, on average 4 years.

Finally we come to the level of qualifications obtained. This was measured on an eight-point scale, as follows: (0) none, (1) general, (2) minor, (3) City and Guilds, ONC, A-level etc., (4) minor professional institution, (5) HNC, (6) major professional institution, (7) degree. Forty per cent had no qualifications, and the median for those that had came between the third and fourth categories.

When we consider the relationship between background and education, our results (Table 3.1) are in line with the many studies which point to the importance of the father's occupational status for the son's educational attainment. We would not necessarily expect to find this, and certainly would expect a weaker relationship than in the population at large. Since our sample is limited to non-manual workers, those with low-status fathers have been upwardly mobile and hence typically better educated than those from similar backgrounds who have been excluded.

We have included both the straightforward manual/non-manual dichotomy and our own more finely graded measure of occupational status. Clearly, the two are closely related ($r = 0.66$), but each has an independent effect. That is, even when allowance is made for father's status, educational attainment is still affected by the manual/non-manual distinction. Similarly, when the latter is allowed for there is a contribution from the status gradations within each group – in the case of manual workers this is primarily the difference between unskilled and skilled workers.

Attendance at a selective school is slightly better related to the father being a non-manual worker than it is to his overall occupational status. However, the balance begins to shift for the number of years spent at school beyond the minimum and it is the first measure alone (although this, of course, includes a manual/non-manual element) which determines the number of years spent in full-time further education. In each case those with higher-status fathers are in the more favourable situation, and it is worth noting, especially in view of the nature of our sample, that the effect is maintained to the level of further education even when the previous influence on school attainment has been allowed for. There is no continuing effect, though, on either of the part-time modes of further education, or on the level of qualification obtained.

Of course, as we proceed through the various levels of the educa-

TABLE 3.1 *The process of educational attainment (path coefficients)*

	Age	Community of origin	Father non-manual	Father's status	Type of school	Years at school	Further education Full-time	Part-time Day	Evening	Residual
Type of school	-0.17	–	0.18	0.13						0.94
Years at school		-0.05	0.12	0.14	0.51					0.78
Further education										
Full-time	-0.11	–	–	0.12	–	0.30				0.92
Part-time (day)	-0.28	–	–	–	–	-0.06				0.96
Part-time (evening)	0.11	0.10	–	–	–	–				0.99
Qualifications	-0.09	–	–	–	0.11	0.20	0.47	0.26	0.29	0.69

tional system, each succeeding level tends to be determined most by the ones preceding. Those who have been to a selective school are likely to have stayed on longer, and those who have done so are likely to have spent more time in full-time further education. The interesting exceptions to this are the two forms of part-time further education. Staying on longer at school has a small effect on years of part-time evening education, but in a negative, that is a depressive direction. Consumption of these aspects of education is otherwise largely unrelated to the normally significant features of social background. Nevertheless, it is clear that they are important in the attainment of qualifications, together directly accounting for about the same amount of variance as full-time further education.

The increasing availability of day-release and similar forms of part-time day education almost certainly accounts for the large negative effect that age has on years spent at this. Older respondents are, on the contrary, likely to have spent more years in part-time evening education. Whether an increase in the availability of grammar school places similarly accounts for the fact that older persons are less likely to have attended a selective school is more doubtful. It almost certainly does have an effect but is unlikely to be the only factor. It is probable that our older respondents include a number who have been intra-generationally mobile upwards, although the correlation between age and father's occupational status is weak ($r = -0.04$). It is also true that age has a negative effect on the number of years spent in full-time further education, and on level of qualifications. It may be that this reflects greater bureaucratisation of non-manual work over time, and the consequent greater emphasis on formal qualifications, as well as the growth in technical and professional occupations where competence is more formally assessed.

The size of the respondent's community of origin generally has only a small effect on educational attainment. Those from the largest communities, in particular, are less likely to have stayed on at school for as long beyond the minimum leaving age. On the other hand they are likely to have spent more time in part-time evening education, probably reflecting greater availability.

There are three other aspects of background which occur as determinants in some of the later analyses and which can usefully be dealt with here. They are geographical mobility, association membership and activity, and the status of the respondent's friends and neighbours. Two variables are used as indicators of geographical mobility: the distance that the individual has moved from his community of upbringing and the number of times he has moved house since obtaining his first job. Neither is a perfect indicator of mobility, since it is possible for an individual to have made one long move from his community of upbringing, in his youth, and since then to have been virtually immobile, whilst equally it is possible for someone to have moved house a large number of times, but only within a restricted area. In fact the relationship between these two variables is only moderate ($r = 0.26$) and anyway our respondents do not appear to be particularly mobile geographically. Of course there are a few who have moved considerable distances but, excluding those coming from overseas, the average distance moved since childhood is only 54 miles, while 36 per cent are still living within 5 miles of where they grew up. As well as the fact of being born abroad, which naturally is most closely related to distance moved, most of the other influences are as one would expect. Older persons tend to have moved furthest ($p = 0.09$), as do those who have spent a longer time at school or in full-time further education ($p = 0.21$ and $p = 0.14$ respectively). Having a higher-status father ($p = 0.11$) and having been brought up in a smaller community ($p = -0.06$) are also linked with having moved further, as is having a greater number of dependents ($p = 0.12$). On the other hand, ownership of one's own home has a constraining influence on mobility.

The low average mobility of our sample may be seen even more clearly in the fact that the mean number of moves is only 1.8. As we would expect the number increases with age ($p = 0.28$), and no doubt many of the younger men, at least, will make more moves in the future. However, it is somewhat surprising that at the time of the research, and bearing in mind that the mean age was nearly 40, 56 per cent had moved no more than once, if at all. In addition to age, several of the educational variables, particularly time spent in further education, make a contribution, almost certainly because of their relationship to the individual's own achieved occupational status. Here also, being married, as well as having a larger number of dependents, tends to be associated with greater mobility, at least between homes ($p = 0.10$ in both cases).

The remaining background variables that we shall consider are 'background' only in the sense that they do not relate to the current, immediate work experience of the individual. The first of these relate to the degree of involvement, as measured by frequency of attendance, in various kinds of associations. We have distinguished between religious, political, and other associations, the last covering mainly sporting and recreational activities. Some 39 per cent of respondents do not attend any such association even as little as once a year. The fewest (5 per cent) attend meetings of any kind of political body, and they attend on average, about once every 2 weeks. Rather more (16 per cent) attend religious meetings, on average 41 times a year, but most popular are the various other kinds of association. There are still 47 per cent who do not attend at all. On the other hand those who do, who are more likely to be unmarried, average nearly one meeting a week.

Our main concern with the status of the individual's neighbours and of his friends is in their use, in the subsequent analysis, as indicators of important social referents that the individual may have. We would expect that the kinds of people that he chooses as friends and that he has around him as neighbours are likely to be significant in influencing his perceptions of, and expectations regarding, his own position. We asked respondents for the occupations of their four nearest neighbours, and of four people with whom they were friendly outside work. These occupations were scored and, in each case, an average taken of the four, or of the total number given, if this was less. The mean status of neighbours at 122, about the level of supervising clerk or office manager, is rather lower than that of our respondents, while that of friends (145) is very close. In large part this latter is to be expected, given the way in which the occupational status score was constructed, with the scale being derived from a comparison of friendship choices between the different occupational groups. Although both of these may be regarded as background factors they are certainly not independent of present location and rewards. Accordingly we will postpone further consideration to the next section.

SOCIAL LOCATION AND REWARDS

Let us now return to the major question with which we are concerned in the early part of this chapter, that is the relationship between social background and rewards. Differently put, we must examine the processes of individual attainment and of how those in our sample come to occupy their position in the structure of reward distribution.

We shall be primarily concerned with two major rewards, the individual's earnings and the status of his present job. We do, however, have information also on the individual's first job and his first job in his present employing organisation. In both cases these occupations have been given a score on our scale. The mean score on first job is 108, just a little higher than the average of respondents' fathers, and corresponds to about the level of clerks. The average for the first job in the firm already shows an increase on this, to 125, about the level of supervisory clerks and office managers, and the score on present job shows a further increase to 152, somewhere between draughtsmen and laboratory technicians. It is higher for those in the public sector (187), and correspondingly lower for those in private employment (144). Bearing in mind that in some cases two of these jobs, and possibly all three, are the same and have been held for only a short period, it is clear that many of our non-manual respondents have enjoyed a considerable degree of upward occupational mobility, both over their whole career and within their present employment. This fact, either as personal experience or as awareness of a general situation, is likely to be of great significance to most respondents.

The relative importance of educational factors in determining occupational position is clearly shown in our results (see Table 3.2). In looking at first job it makes more sense to exclude part-time education, since this occurs subsequently. Then, at this stage, the most important influence is from the number of years spent in full-time further education. In addition there are important effects from the number of years over the minimum spent at school, type of school attended and level of qualifications obtained. The direct effect at this stage from father's occupational status is small but still significant. In line with our suggestion earlier, we find that older respondents are likely to have had a first job which was of lower status.

Following individuals through to their first job in the firm, we find, naturally enough, that there is a substantial carry-over from their first job. Apart from this, by far the largest contribution comes from level of qualifications. This additional direct effect is actually greater than was that on the status of the individual's first job. This may in part be because some individuals move to jobs which are more in line with their qualifications than is their first, but is almost certainly more a result of many acquiring qualifications after beginning employment. As we saw earlier, part-time further education is of considerable importance in the acquisition of qualifications. This is an aspect of occupational attainment which, despite some efforts to bring it to attention (Lee, 1966), has largely been underplayed in previous studies

TABLE 3.2 Social location and rewards and social background (path coefficients)

	Age	Father's status	Type of school	Years at school	Full-time further education	Qualifications	Part-time (day) further education	Number of dependents	Married	Number of moves	First job status	First job in firm status	Service in firm	Present job status	Residual
First job status	-0.13	0.07	0.10	0.19	0.26	0.20									0.77
First job in firm status	-0.04	0.05	0.05	-	-	0.34	0.04	-	-	0.14	0.41				0.68
Present job status	0.07 *(-)	-	0.06 (0.08)	-	-	0.23 (0.26)	0.05 (0.05)	-	-	0.05 (0.08)	-	0.57 (0.45)	-		0.64 (0.70)
Income	0.22	-	-	0.07	-	0.20	-	0.16	0.10	0.09	-	0.12	0.19	0.27	0.69

* Values adjusted to allow for jobs held for short period—see text.

(see, however, Raffe, 1979; Blackburn, Stewart and Prandy, 1980). There is evidence, also, that the more geographically mobile tend to secure higher-status positions, in that the number of moves appears to have a fairly strong influence. Clearly this should not be seen as a mechanical effect, but rather as an indication that willingness to move is important. To some extent the effect may operate in the reverse direction, with movement to a higher-status job leading to a change of residence.

A problem with using the whole sample for this analysis is that the carry-over effect is in part inflated by the fact that for those of our respondents who have stayed within the same company the first job and the first job in this firm are necessarily identical. A number of these will be younger respondents for whom the two 'events' are not only coincident but also fairly recent. In fact, if we try to make a partial allowance for this, by restricting the analysis to those who have either changed between their first job and their first job in their present firm, or who have been employed for at least 10 years, thus allowing them a reasonable period in which to move, we do not find any major changes other than that the carry-over effect from the first job necessarily diminishes ($p = 0.33$) and that there is a slight increase in the influence from qualifications ($p = 0.37$).

As we move on to consider the status of the individual's present job, we find that by far the most important determinant is again that of his previous employment, and as in the case of his first job in his present employing organisation level of qualifications is by far the most important of the other influences. These results are for the total sample, and again there is the problem that arises because some people have been only a short time with their present employer. Here, however, we can restrict the analysis to the 73 per cent who have either changed from their first job in the firm to their present job, or who have spent at least 10 years with their current employer. When this is done the effect from the status of the first job in the company declines, while that from level of qualifications increases. Those who move house more often still tend to fare better in terms of their present job, though in this case it is rather more likely that the direction of causal effect has been wrongly specified. Finally, we note that those who attended a selective school were further aided in the achievement of higher-status jobs; a minor effect, but interesting in that it operates at so many removes.

We have, then, a definite process of generally upward movement to the present job, and the influence of different factors must be seen in this light. At each stage it is the recent past that is most important. Background factors such as education are directly important early in a career, then their effect becomes progressively more indirect as the career develops. However, formal qualifications are something of an exception in that they first increase and subsequently retain a substantial direct influence, though this must be understood, in part at least, as a result of their continuing acquisition in the course of a career. We see also that the geographically mobile tend to be successful, more so at the point of entry to the firm than to the present job. It seems such mobility takes place more between firms than within them, and in any case is less important in the determination of income than the length of time with the same firm. However this cannot be taken as indicating that advancement is faster for those who stay, particularly when we realise that overwhelmingly the most important determinant of present status is status on joining the firm. Finally, we should note that despite this general movement upward, which necessarily takes some time, the effect of age on present occupational status is comparatively weak. This suggests strongly that our sample includes either a number of young, higher-status, or old, lower-status people, or most probably both. It seems that our sample does tend to under-represent the very highest levels, and thus the men in the older age ranges who have been most successful. However, we should not make too much of this as part of the explanation is the lack of discrimination within conventional occupational categories, and as we shall see the relationship is much higher with income.

Turning, now, to the individual's current income the average figure is £1664 per annum – slightly lower (£1628) in private employment than in public (£1816). These may be compared to a national average at about that time of £1528 for all adult males and £1856 for adult male non-manual workers (DEP, 1970). Within the organisation the individual's earnings are of course strongly related to his hierarchical position. Although it does not overcome the problems of inter-firm comparisons our measure of occupational status is the best available indicator of hierarchical position. This implies that we take income as dependent upon status, whereas most theories of stratification make the opposite assumption. There is a substantial effect on income from occupational status. However it is very interesting that in addition there are a number of quite large independent influences from other factors. Foremost amongst these are age and level of qualifications. It is perhaps worth noting that these three factors are sufficient to account for the higher average earnings in the public sector. In fact when they are allowed for, those in the latter appear as underpaid.

The importance of qualifications is somewhat surprising in view of the fact that our measure of occupational status already allows higher scores to the more highly qualified professional groups. What appears to be the case is that within broad occupational categories there are significant benefits in terms of income from the possession of qualifications. The fact that age has an effect is perhaps less surprising, in so far as it represents a general tendency for some degree of age-grading in income, as well as reflecting the fact that within a number of occupational categories, in particular the professional group, there are considerable differences in income levels. However, that it is the most important effect, apart from occupational status, and that it is further reinforced by the influence of length of service in the firm is very significant. This high degree of built-in benefit for the older and longer-service employees is not always as fully appreciated as it should be.

The only educational variable to have any important effect, apart from level of qualifications, is the number of years spent at school. To what extent this represents a degree of discrimination in favour of grammar- and, perhaps, public-school boys, and to what extent it simply represents a return to educational attainment or ability which is not directly reflected in qualifications, is not clear.

That there are still some minor returns to geographical mobility, given occupational status, is shown by the influence of the number of moves that the individual has made. The status of his first job in the firm also has a small but significant effect. It appears that movement to gain higher pay can be successful. The fact that those who are married and those with more dependents have higher incomes may also reflect success in seeking financial rewards or it may be due to employers' preferences. Among manual workers men with these responsibilities are more likely to have economistic orientations and to be regarded as more reliable employees (Blackburn and Mann, 1979) but it is not clear how far this is true for the better-paid non-manual workers.

The most important of the relationships that have been dealt with in the first part of this chapter can be summarised with the help of a path diagram (Figure 3.1). The contribution of education, in various forms, is shown very clearly. All – apart from those involving part-time education – have an effect on the status level that is attained in the first job. Thereafter, all of their influence is mediated through the level of qualifications, of which part-time education is now an

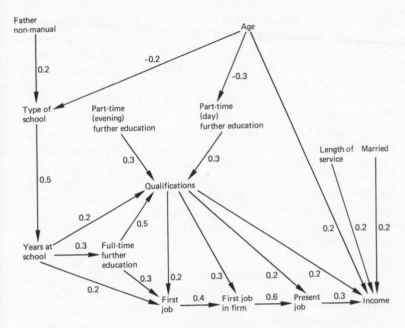

FIGURE 3.1 *Simplified path representation of determination of social location*

important determinant. This factor itself has a major direct influence on all three successive career stages, and on income.

The advantages of having a higher-status father are mainly worked out in full-time education, and there is no subsequent influence of any importance. Age, however, continues to have an effect right through the model, not only on certain features of educational experience, but also on the status of the first job and on current income.

Apart from the acquisition of qualifications through part-time study and, to a much lesser extent, the willingness to move as opportunities occur, there is a regular progression of occupational movement and attainment of income, which is relatively highly determined and is set in train early in the individual's life. Because of the regularity of this process it is more fruitful to apply the concept of a 'career' than the usual idea of occupational mobility (for a fuller consideration of this point see Stewart, Prandy and Blackburn, 1980).

Before finishing this section we now can deal briefly with the question – deferred from the last – of the determinants of the status of neighbours and friends. Given the relationship between friendship choices and the way in which our scale of occupational status was derived, it is hardly surprising that the respondent's own occupation is the major determinant of that of his friends ($p = 0.29$). It is worth noting, though, that there is an additional effect from income ($p = 0.13$) and that in the case of neighbours not only is income more important than it is for friends ($p = 0.25$), but it is also a stronger influence than is the individual's own status ($p = 0.13$). This is interesting in so far as many would regard residential location as itself a good indicator of social status, but we need not be too surprised at the greater importance of income. Many high-status occupations, the professions in particular, are relatively low-paid at the younger ages, and their incumbents are thus likely to live in cheaper houses with lower-status neighbours. However, the influence of income on the status of a man's friends appears to suggest that not only can high-status neighbours be 'bought', but in addition, perhaps through choice of lifestyle, high-status friends. Of course this fails to take account of the fact that friends and neighbours are often the same people, and if we make the assumption that it is more likely that friendships develop amongst neighbours than that people move to live next to their friends, then we can to an extent allow for this. What we then find is that although the effect on the status of friends from his own status is very slightly reduced ($p = 0.28$), that from income declines considerably ($p = 0.07$). The influence of a man's neighbours is quite strong ($p = 0.20$), though still not as great as that of his own job. Most of the other relationships are substantially similar, though a little weaker.

PERCEPTIONS OF REWARDS

In this section we shall deal, in turn, with the five major rewards that we argued in the first chapter were most significant for the individual in the employment situation. In the case of two of them, income and the status of his present job, we shall be extending the discussion that we have already undertaken, and we shall be able to compare the individual's perceptions of his position with our objective measures of it. For three of the rewards, however, we do not have any objective measures with which to compare perceptions; these are intrinsic job rewards, social interaction and security.

We shall also include in this section an aspect of work which, while in itself not strictly a reward, is certainly related to the future improvement in rewards, that is promotion. As we argued in the first chapter, none of our rewards is simple, in that for example increased income may be salient for the individual not as greater buying power but as an indication of recognition and a higher status. Promotion as a reward is even more complex, since as has been said it usually involves an increase in several other rewards, and may in itself be taken as an indication, again, of recognition, and thus serve to enhance the individual's self-esteem. Conversely, of course, the lack of promotion may not only prove frustrating in itself, but may be taken by the individual as a reflection on his worth. The difficulty in dealing with promotion is compounded by the fact that it represents one possible strategy for the alleviation of a situation of discrepancy between actual and expected rewards. However, we must leave a consideration of this aspect to a later chapter.

We have two purposes in measuring perceptions of rewards. The first relates to those rewards for which objective measures are not available, where the individual's perceptions are taken as indicating the actual rewards. To some extent this is a disadvantage since, as we pointed out earlier, there is a problem in that in looking at the relationship between background and perceptions, it is not clear how far we are looking at background factors as determinants of the rewards secured, rather than of the perceptions of them. However, to state the problem in these terms is already to indicate that there is a considerable difficulty in looking at the objective nature of rewards. Many of them are of course difficult to quantify. How, for example, could one think of measuring the extent of social interaction rewards? The problem goes further than this, however. To say that a man earns so many pounds per annum is apparently a quite objective statement, and income appears to be a perfectly easily measurable quantity. However, even in an objective sense income, simply in terms of numbers of pounds, means very little except in a broader context of the distribution of earnings throughout a society and of factors such as the cost of living. Ideas such as the cost of living, though, already introduce important social elements into the equation, since it involves ideas about style of life, culturally approved objects of consumption and so on.

This brings us to our second purpose, which is to set the perceptions in a meaningful social context. To understand not only how rewards are perceived, but even more the evaluations that stem from these perceptions, it is important to place them within a frame of reference. Where appropriate we have used three groups for comparative reference: people doing the same sort of job as the respondent, typical or average manual workers, and top managers. We have also used the two contexts of the employing organisation and the wider society. The point is clearly illustrated in the case of income. For the individual, as we noted above, his own earnings have no meaning outside the cultural context of their use, and judgements about them must be made in relation to his perceptions of the earnings of significant others. Of course this includes his perceptions of his own earnings in the past, but these would be difficult to measure and can anyway be approached indirectly through, for example, job history. More interesting are his perceptions of contemporaries. Status and security lend themselves to similar approaches. For other rewards, however, such comparisons are less appropriate. They may not make much sense, as in the case of the individual trying to compare his promotion prospects with those of top management, and the individual may have only a limited basis for comparison. There is little by which to judge the level of rewards from the intrinsic aspects of the job, for example, except on the basis of some comparison, but this is likely to be implicit and involve levels seen as possible in other situations rather than perceptions of the rewards of other people, apart from stereotypes like assembly-line work. Our approach has been to obtain such data on perceptions as is meaningful for each type of reward, tempered by the inevitable consideration of what was practicable.

Income

It may seem somewhat strange to consider asking questions on people's perceptions of their own income. In most cases one would expect the individual to have a good idea of what his actual earnings are, and to treat his reporting of these as 'perceptions' is being over-particular. Indeed this is the view we adopted. We did ask for the individual's basic earnings, but this figure is treated as an objective measure, and one which we have already used in our analysis. In addition we asked about his own additional earnings and those of other members of his household. Of course some respondents may have lied, and some may have made only an approximation where they were unsure of the precise figures. However, it does seem reasonable to assume that in this case there is no particular problem in letting the perceptions stand for the actual reward.

The 'perceptions' of income we are concerned with relate not to the respondent, but to others who constitute the frame of reference within which to set his own actual earnings. The most obvious point of reference is that of people doing similar work. Subsequently we shall refer to this as his own occupational group, using both of the last two words only in a very loose sense. Thus, for our measurement of perceived income we asked each respondent what he thought were the average earnings of a man in his position doing broadly the same kind of work as himself. We distinguished between someone in the same company and those working elsewhere. Since we were interested in the individual's comparative perceptions, we asked a similar question regarding an 'average manual worker' and an 'average top manager', again for both within the company and outside it.

The average annual income reported by our respondents is, as we said earlier, £1664. Those that they judge as similar to themselves, within the same company, are believed to average about the same – £1669. However, when they look outside their own company they believe that, on average, people elsewhere doing work similar to their own earn £1733 per annum. It seems that our respondents have a sense that they are less well-paid than they would be elsewhere, although possibly their conceptions of 'people like themselves' in other areas of employment may tend to be biased in an upward direction.

Naturally enough the major determinant of respondents' perceptions of what is earned by people doing similar jobs to themselves in the same company is their own actual income ($p = 0.95$). Beyond this we are essentially considering those characteristics which lead an individual to believe that those whom he considers comparable to himself are being paid more or less than he is. In fact the only other effect is that those who have more dependents ($p = 0.03$) tend to give a higher figure. When it is the income of their own occupational group outside the company, in the wider society, that is being assessed, there is still a strong effect from their own earnings ($p = 0.85$). The only other influences of any size are that those who have higher-status friends ($p = 0.04$) or are owner-occupiers ($p = 0.03$), and older respondents ($p = 0.03$) tend to give higher estimates of outsiders' salaries.

Rather more interesting than these perceptions, which depend so much on the individual's own income, are his ideas of the earnings of other groups, as represented by an average manual worker and an average top manager, both within the company and outside it. In the case of manual workers, those employed within the company are seen as earning rather more than do those without, an average of £1145 as against £1109. These estimates are some way below the published figure for annual earnings of adult manual workers at around the time of our survey, which was about £1362 (DEP, 1970). By contrast, our respondents believe that top managers within their own company are lower paid than those outside – £4227 as compared with £4674. In both cases the standard deviations are very large, which may reflect the vagueness of our term top manager. Possibly many people believed that the upper limit for this category went higher in the wider society than it did within their own company.

In marked contrast to the cases of the earnings of those at their own level we have not been very successful in accounting for perceptions of the earnings of these other groups. As far as within-company comparisons are concerned the most important determinants are the individual's own income and the type of school that he went to. The higher his own earnings, the higher he believes the earnings of both manual workers ($p = 0.17$) and top managers ($p = 0.13$) to be. This seems to be mainly the effect of an individual tendency to assess others in terms of one's own position, a kind of halo effect, since it cannot be accounted for by differences between employing establishments.

The effect of the type of school that the respondent attended is opposite in the two cases; that is, those who went to a selective school give lower estimates of the earnings of manual workers ($p = -0.13$), but higher ones of those of top managers ($p = 0.12$). In the latter case this effect is backed up by a further one from the number of years spent at school beyond the minimum ($p = 0.07$). A similar pattern is found in the case of owner-occupation. That is, those who own their own houses tend to see manual workers as earnings less ($p = -0.08$) and top managers more ($p = 0.06$). Older respondents tend to give lower estimates of the earnings of both manual workers ($p = -0.14$) and top managers ($p = -0.06$), although this is largely offset by positive influences from length of service in the firm ($p = 0.10$ and $p = 0.09$ respectively). Some of these effects, however, seem to be explained by the kinds of establishments in which different people are employed. Where more men with a selective school background are employed there is a general agreement on the lower pay of manual workers, and the higher pay of top managers. Thus the results seem to reflect the actual situation, rather than individual differences. The same is true of the belief by longer-service employees that manual workers and top managers earn more.

Even less can be explained of the perceptions of two groups in the wider society, especially manual workers. The patterns of influence are similar, but weaker. Thus, top managers tend to be seen as earning more by those whose own incomes are higher ($p = 0.13$), by those who attended a selective school ($p = 0.07$) and stayed on for more years beyond the minimum ($p = 0.09$), and by owner-occupiers ($p = 0.07$). The individual's own earnings do not affect his view of what manual workers in general earn, the only influence being the mainly counteracting ones of age ($p = -0.09$) and length of service in the firm ($p = 0.06$).

These results, it should be emphasised, do not for the most part reflect on the accuracy of our respondents' perceptions, but essentially on the existence of systematic differences. Only in the case of income is the question of accuracy to some extent involved. Thus, at one extreme, perceptions of the earnings of their own occupational group in the company are naturally determined by respondents' own incomes. At the other, perceptions of manual workers' earnings in the wider society are not even affected by inter-company variation.

Status

Status is necessarily a relative reward, and not one that most people could quantify in any meaningful way. We decided to adopt a graphical approach to its measurement which would enable respondents to convert general notions of social distance into spatial terms. This required, for simplicity and comparability, our prior specification of the 'space' together with points of reference. Both the space and the points are, to an extent, arbitrary, and may not correspond with those of the individual. Nevertheless, in practice few people found them meaningless, and almost all were able to respond.

What we did to measure perceptions of status was to present the respondent with a horizontal line with 'manual worker' indicated towards one end and 'top manager' towards the other, with the comment that 'occupations differ in the amount of prestige or social standing that they have' and that we should like his views on his comparative position. He was then asked to mark whereabouts on the line he thought that his particular job 'would be put by most people (a) in this company, and (b) in the community at large'. In this case there is little sense in distinguishing the individual's perception of his own status from that of workers in the same position, and asking about his particular job combined the two. We do, of course, have an objective measure of status, at least in the community at large, but of a very different kind. Given our emphasis in constructing that measure on the relational aspects of status, it is perhaps inconsistent

TABLE 3.3 *Influences on perceptions of status and security (path coefficients)*

Perceptions	Father non-manual	Type of school	Full-time further education	Qualifications	Married	Friends' status	Neigh-bours' status	First job status	Service in firm	Present job status	Income	Extra earnings	Subord-inates: time	Residual
Company status	0.05	–	–	0.06	–	0.06	0.05	–	–	0.16	0.33	–0.05	0.07	0.83
Society status	–	–	–	–	–	–	0.06	–	–	0.22	0.27	–0.05	0.09	0.88
Security:														
Own level	–	–	–0.07	–	–	–	–	–	–	0.08	–	–	–	1.00
Manual worker	0.06	0.12	–	–	–0.07	–	0.12	–	–	0.09	–	–	–	0.96
Top manager	–	–	–	0.09	–	0.07	0.09	0.07	0.08	0.08	–	–	–	0.96

to question respondents in terms of what is essentially a reputational approach. However, it seemed to us that few respondents would be able unambiguously to conceptualise status in terms of relationships, and that in so far as they could, it would be in terms of social standing. Moreover, it would consequently be this latter aspect which would be most significant for them, and it would be in relation to it that they could distinguish between their position within the company and in the wider society, and between what they saw as their actual situation and what they believed it ought to be (a question that we take up in the next chapter).

Possible scores on the two items range from 0 to 60 (with manual worker scored 5 and top manager 55), and we find that the mean of the responses is, in fact, very close to the middle of this line. The average score on where the respondent believed that his job was placed by other people in the community at large was 29.7, whereas the corresponding score for his job in the company was somewhat lower at 28.7. The two scores are, as we might expect, well related ($r = 0.71$). One point emerging here is that our respondents see themselves standing well above manual workers in status. It is true that this may be partially an artefact of our method, which was likely to discourage respondents from placing themselves below manual workers, but in fact the great majority placed themselves a long way above.

Looking at the determinants of perceived status (Table 3.3), what is most interesting is the relative influence of income and of our measure of the individual's occupational status. The former is better related than the latter to perceptions of both company and community status. Since the two perceptions are so well correlated we would expect the effects on them to be quite similar. Although this is so, there are nevertheless some differences. The effect of income is slightly lower on status in the community than on status in the company, whereas the reverse is the case for the influence of our measure of occupational status. These differences are small, but in the direction that one would anticipate. Within the company most people probably associate status with the authority hierarchy, and since this largely determines also the income hierarchy, the two are strongly related. In the wider community though, where different status effects would operate more, we would expect income to be less important. The lower effect of our 'status' measure is almost certainly due to its general nature. It groups all members of occupations together, young and old, low and high earners. Although there is some sense in regarding professions with career structures as social entities, the fact that our measures of status perception tap specific positions in employment hierarchies rather than careers means status and perceived status are not measuring identical experiences. Income is likely to be much more clearly associated with present position.

The influence of the authority hierarchy within the firm comes out in another way, in that the more time that an individual has spent with subordinates in an average day, the higher he believes his status both in the company and in the society to be. There are also positive influences in the former instance from the status of both the man's friends and his neighbours, but surprisingly only the second of these has any significant effect on his perceptions of his status in the wider society. Somewhat unexpected, too, is the influence on each of the occupational status of the father, where one would anticipate some carry-over effect from father to son in the wider community, but much less in the more restricted area of the firm. In fact no such effect is apparent in the former case, while there is a small tendency for those with non-manual fathers to believe they have higher status in the latter. Here, of course, it is important to remember that we are considering the remaining direct effect, after the indirect effects through education, occupation and so on have been allowed for.

Security

In the case of security we have chosen to approach perceptions only from a relative or comparative point of view, without also attempting to measure some absolute level as we did for income and status. Not only would the latter be difficult, it would almost certainly be of little use, since this is an area where it is likely that social comparison processes operate very significantly. The individual can to some extent assess how secure his job is, but except when redundancy is an imminent threat it is far easier, and far more meaningful, for him to assess the degree of his personal job security when compared to that of other groups. In order to determine whether the comparison with groups higher or lower in the hierarchy was more significant for the individual, we asked him to compare his job security with that of an average manual worker and an average top manager. In addition, we were interested in his perception of his position when compared to that of other people in a similar situation to his own. The question that we asked was how the respondent would rate the security of his job, compared with each of these three groups, and responses were recorded on lines which this time ran from 'much more secure' (scored 22), through 'more secure' (17), 'about the same' (12), and so on to 'much less secure' (7).

Individual-level factors are not very useful in predicting the individual's perceptions of his degree of security. Almost nothing can be explained of his comparison with others doing similar jobs to his own, where the average score was 14 (that is, a little better than 'about the same'). However there is a small tendency for those of higher occupational status to consider themselves as more secure, and for those who have had more years of full-time further education to see themselves as worse off. The comparison with manual workers is on average more favourable (17), considerably more so for those in the public sector (20) than for those in private employment (16). Those who have attended a selective school, and those whose own occupational status and that of their neighbours is higher, are likely to see their own situation as more advantageous, while those who are married and those whose own fathers were manual workers tend to take a less favourable view.

Respondents in private industry see themselves as having much the same level of security as top managers (13); those in the public sector rather more (17). It is again those of higher occupational status and those living in higher-status neighbourhoods, in so far as this is indicated by their immediate neighbours, who rate their own position most favourably, as also do those with higher levels of qualifications and those with longer service in the firm (Table 3.3).

Intrinsic job

The measurement of intrinsic job characteristics raises several difficult problems, even a partial solution of which involves considerable time and effort (Turner and Lawrence, 1965; Blackburn and Mann, 1979). Unfortunately, in this study it was not possible for us to gather any detailed information on the nature of each respondent's job, so that we could not consider making use of those objective rating schemes that are available. Instead we were forced to rely entirely on the individual's own perceptions. In a practical sense the latter are easier to obtain, but are clearly less valid. Moreover, given the difficulties and the time in the interview that we could allow, we decided not to attempt to get detailed individual ratings of 'objective' features of the job, but to rely solely on reactions to more general statements. This means, of course, that responses are affected by a number of personal factors in addition to those which make up the objective characteristics of the job, but the work of Turner and Lawrence suggests that such responses are quite strongly related to the latter. A further drawback compared with some of the rewards that we have previously considered is that we were unable to devise a method by which we could ask people to make assessments within a particular framework of comparison.

What we did was to present respondents with a number of statements and to ask them to record their degree of agreement or disagreement on a five-point scale. Factor analysis of the responses suggested that there were two sets of items that related well to one another, so within each set we added together the scores on the individual items, weighting them in such a way as to obtain the best estimate of the underlying factor. Three items went to make up one composite measure, which we shall refer to as the degree of control that the individual has over the job, or simply 'control'. They are listed below, with their factor loadings (that is their correlation with the factor), from which it is clear that the third item is the most representative of the set, and the first item the least.

'A person who wanted to make his own decisions would be discouraged here' (-0.46).
'I am completely free to organise my work as I want to' (0.73).
'I feel that I am my own boss in most matters' (0.84).

The second set of four items make up a composite measure which, as can be seen from the items and their factor loadings below, is concerned with the individual's use of his abilities in his job. The items are:
'Anyone with reasonable qualifications could learn to do my job in about one month' (-0.73).
'My job provides me with excellent opportunities to increase my knowledge and abilities' (0.60).
'My job uses only a small part of my abilities' (-0.65).
'I almost always do the same thing in my job; there is hardly any variety' (-0.54).

As can be seen, no single one of these items is as highly related to the overall construct as is the third item of the previous set, but all of the correlations are of a reasonably high order.

One would not expect these two aspects of intrinsic job reward to be

TABLE 3.4 *Influences on perceptions of intrinsic job (path coefficients)*

Perceptions	Age	Married	Service in firm	Income	Present job status	Subordinates		Superiors		Others: Number	Residual
						Time	Number	Time	Number		
Use of abilities	−0.13	0.09	0.07	0.31	0.16	0.05	0.10	0.10	—	0.06	0.89
Control	—	0.11	—	0.20	—	0.10	—	—	−0.05	0.09	0.95

independent of one another, and indeed they are not. However the correlation between them is relatively low ($r = 0.36$). In terms of the five categories of the original items, the means of these two variables correspond to a position just on the favourable side of the middle, 'neither agree nor disagree', category.

The major determinant of these perceptions of both control and use of abilities is the respondent's income (Table 3.4). Obviously in this case when speaking of income as a determinant what is meant is that income serves as an indicator of a variety of factors relating to occupational position and to location in the reward distribution and authority structure. However, as with perceptions of status, it is interesting that the status of the respondent's present job has a smaller influence on his perceptions of the use of his abilities, and no significant one on his perceptions of control. Once again the gross nature of the scale, allowing as it does for very different career points to be scored equally, must contribute to this result. That use of abilities, but not control, is directly affected, probably reflects the fact that professional occupations tend to score higher on our scale.

The importance of the authority structure of the enterprise is further shown in the effects of those variables relating to social interaction with others in the firm. The more time spent with sub-ordinates and the more other people (neither superiors nor sub-ordinates) that are seen in the course of the job, the more favourable are perceptions of control. With respect to use of abilities these factors also have an effect, but there is a stronger one from the number of subordinates seen. In contrast, the more superiors that are seen the lower is the perceived degree of control. Use of abilities, though, seems to be greater the more time that is spent with superiors.

Background factors generally appear to have little direct influence on intrinsic job rewards. Those who are married enjoy, or think that they enjoy, both greater control and use of their abilities at work. Otherwise, only the latter are affected; older respondents generally have lower perceptions, although this effect is to some extent cancelled out by the fact that those with longer service in the firm tend to have higher ones. What this suggests is that, as we would expect, longer-service employees are in the more rewarding jobs amongst those that cannot be differentiated by criteria such as income and status, but that older workers have moved into less rewarding ones. This interpretation is supported by the fact that the lower perceptions seem to be accounted for by differences between establishments.

Since with measures of the kind that we have used it is impossible entirely to separate perceptions from the expectations that people have regarding their jobs, it could be that longer-service employees only think of their position more favourably because their expectations are lower. However, one would anticipate a similar, rather than an opposing, effect from age in this case. More generally the relative unimportance of background variables, as compared with those concerned fairly directly with a position in the authority and reward structure, suggests that we have been successful in measuring the actual job characteristics, uncontaminated by variations in expectations.

Social interaction

Social interaction rewards are taken to be of two kinds. There are firstly those concerned with the individual's relationship to his work group and others with whom he works. Secondly there is that social interaction which specifically involves the man's superiors and the relationships that he, and others in the work group, have with them. As may have been noted, we did collect information on the number of superiors, subordinates and others seen during the normal working day, and the amount of time spent with them, but our concern in looking at perceptions was to concentrate on the individual's view of the quality of these different interactions. We did ask respondents to rate their job on the extent to which it allowed them to talk to other people, on a five-point scale ranging from 'very often' to 'very rarely', but the main measure of perceptions of social interaction is made up of two items. The first relates to the extent to which they see the people they work with as forming a team, and the second concerns the extent to which they think that their own group compares well with others 'in the way that people stick together and help each other'. Both again were on a five-point scale, and the two scores were simply added to give the composite. The mean score is slightly on the neutral side of moderately favourable.

In approaching the measurement of perceptions of superiors we deliberately concentrated on the most significant – the respondent's immediate superior. Seven items were used to contruct a composite measure by means of factor analysis. One was simply a five-point scale of how well the respondent thought that he got on with his superior, with responses ranging from 'not at all well' to 'extremely well'. Its factor loading was 0.73. The remaining six consisted of statements with which respondents were invited to express their degree of agreement or disagreement. They are given below, and as can be seen are essentially ratings of the superior's performance.

'He is much more helpful than others' (0.76).
'He does not tell me where I stand' (−0.62).
'He knows his job well' (0.55).
'He seldom praises good work' (−0.56).
'He often asks my advice' (0.43).
'He stands up for his staff' (0.71).

The mean score again indicates a moderately favourable position.

Income is the only factor that has any sizeable effect on perceptions of social interaction in the work group, with the better-paid tending also to see themselves as being in more helpful work groups with greater team spirit (Table 3.5). The objective measures are together fairly important. The more time spent with both subordinates and superiors, and the more other people seen during the working day, the more favourable are perceptions.

As far as perceptions of the immediate superior are concerned, there is no doubt that the major influence is from the time spent with him. Those who have greater contact with superiors in general (though much of this is in fact likely to be with their own immediate superior) take a much more favourable view of his performance and their relationship with him. Again, so do the better-paid, and so also do those who are older and who have served longer in the firm. How far these latter effects are due to increased tolerance or more reasonable treatment, and how far to a process of selection through leaving, is impossible to say. Nor can we be certain how far greater contact with superiors is simply due to better liking, but administrative considerations make it likely that the effect was from contact to liking.

Promotion

We have already pointed out some of the problems regarding the treatment of promotion as a reward. Of course, individuals may already have experienced some upward movement, and to this extent have already enjoyed promotion. For the most part, however, promotion chances relate to the future, and while it might in principle be possible to calculate an objective measure this was certainly not feasible for us. So again we rely on individual perceptions, and as with intrinsic job rewards we have not attempted to obtain perceptions of

TABLE 3.5   *Influences on perceptions of social interaction, superior and promotion (path coefficients)*

Perceptions	Age	Type of school	Qualifications	Income	Service in firm	Subordinates		Superiors		Others: number	Residual
						Time	Number	Time	Number		
Social interaction	–	–	–	0.17	0.08	0.09	–	0.08	–	0.09	0.97
Superior	0.08	–	–	0.07	0.07	–	–	0.18	–	0.05	0.97
Promotion	–0.13	–	–	0.17	0.17	–	0.11	–	0.06	–	0.97
'Opportunities outside'	–0.27	–0.05	0.18	–	–	–	–	–	–	–	0.90

comparisons with other groups, mainly because we were doubtful of their relevance. Also, we are concerned with the individual's assessment of his own personal position, not that of people similar to himself. The problem here is that promotion is an individual reward, obtained in competition, rather than shared with others. Respondents would have had considerable difficulty in interpreting similarity in this instance, and in any case it was important to know the individual's own position because of the significance of promotion as a 'strategy' as well as a reward.

To measure perceptions of promotion we began with five items, each with five response categories, relating to various aspects of promotion chances – generally, within and outside the company. As might have been expected these do not all relate well together, so we decided to use one item ('There are many good opportunities for me outside this company') by itself as an indicator, obviously, of outside promotion chances. The remainder were subjected to factor analysis and used to construct a composite measure of perceptions of promotion more directly associated with the present job. The items are:

'In this job I have excellent chances of getting ahead in comparison with other lines of work' (0.69).
'Promotion comes slowly in this company' (-0.54).
'It is not always the best people who are chosen for promotion in this company' (-0.39).
'Chances of getting on in this job are much better than could be reasonably expected' (0.73).

As can be seen from its loading, the third of these items is not very well related to the overall construct. It is clear from the wording that it taps a slightly different aspect of the question of advancement and has an element of evaluation not present in the others. However, despite its low weighting it was thought desirable to retain it. As we have suggested above, there is not a very strong correlation between perceptions of promotion opportunities within the company and those outside it ($r = 0.13$). In fact it is true also that the level of perceived opportunity within the company is higher than that outside. In each case the average response is close to the middle category, but for the former it lies just to the favourable side and for the latter to the unfavourable.

Only one factor leads respondents to have favourable perceptions of their opportunities outside their present company, and that is level of qualifications (Table 3.5). As we would expect, older respondents are more likely to take a pessimistic view of opportunities elsewhere, and in addition to this strong effect from age there is a further one from length of service in the company. The causal direction in this latter case is not entirely clear, since it may be that some respondents have remained in the same company because of what they see as poor prospects outside. For the most part, though, the perceptions of these older and longer-service respondents are no doubt realistic, and we would expect that they are likely to develop feelings of constraint, being obliged to remain in the company because of lack of opportunity elsewhere.

As regards perceptions of internal promotion opportunities, there is again a depressing effect from both age and length of service. Here, though, it is income rather than qualifications which leads to a more optimistic view. Part of the reason for the differences in the two cases is that our measure of promotion opportunities is not simply one of the individual's assessment of his own chances, but includes also his evaluation of promotion within the company as a whole. Also, the items included refer not only to future opportunities but to those which the individual may have enjoyed in the past. So the positive effect of income is due not only to the fact that those with higher earnings expect to rise even further, but that they are aware of the distance that they have already moved. Similar considerations, together with quite realistic perceptions of better internal prospects, may also explain why age has a less depressing effect on general perceptions than on those relating specifically to opportunities outside.

We have considered perceptions of each of the rewards separately but in doing so it has become clear that several of them share significant determinants. Two of these, income and occupational status, are themselves rewards, and naturally have a major influence on the respective perceptions. However, the level of income that the individual enjoys also stands out as important for several other perceptions. The individual's perception of his own status, both in the company and in the wider society, is determined more by his income than by our own measure of occupational status. Furthermore, it is the single most important factor in perceptions of intrinsic job rewards – both control and use of abilities, of promotion, and even of social interaction. Only in the case of perceived security compared with other groups is it not significant, but here occupational status has some effect. In all cases these influences are positive, and it is clear

TABLE 3.6   *Inter-relationships of perceptions (correlation coefficients)*

	Income, own level (company)	Company status	Society status	Security:			Control	Use of abilities	Social interaction	Superior
				Own level	Manual worker	Top manager				
Company status	0.50									
Society status	0.43	0.71								
Security										
Own level	0.05	0.36	0.09							
Manual worker	0.21	0.10	0.20	0.36						
Top manager	0.11	0.25	0.19	0.32	0.38					
Control	0.26	0.30	0.23	0.13	0.10	0.13				
Use of abilities	0.42	0.44	0.36	0.15	0.21	0.25	0.35			
Social interaction	0.18	0.23	0.17	0.08	0.09	0.13	0.32	0.35		
Superior	0.08	0.15	0.11	0.11	0.12	0.10	0.28	0.31	0.42	
Promotion	0.12	0.26	0.19	0.07	0.08	0.10	0.22	0.37	0.21	0.26

that there is a tendency for the different rewards to vary together. Certainly there is little indication of any complementarity, such that less of one reward is compensated by more of another.

This can be seen clearly from Table 3.6, which shows the extent to which the perceptions of rewards vary together. Apart from the high correlation between the two aspects of status, the strongest relationships are among income, status and use of abilities. This last is also quite well related to perceptions of control, social interaction and promotion. Although some of the remaining correlations are quite small, all are positive. The structure of rewards is perceived as basically hierarchical with little scope to choose jobs on the basis of one reward at the expense of another. This implies a situation of general competition for better jobs. However, we must bear in mind that workers are not equally placed for such competition and that the processes of job attainment are not separable from the distribution of rewards.

Overall, the results presented in this chapter suggest a relatively well-ordered progression in which educational attainment, much of it part-time and to some extent determined by social background, leads to progression in terms of occupational level. This movement, however, means not merely improvement in 'prestige' and not only in income in addition, but in security, in the use of the individual's abilities and his degree of control, and even in the rewards that derive from social interaction with colleagues and with superiors. However, in addition to the indication of the way in which rewards of various kinds are distributed, we need to know about the ideas that our respondents have about the rewards that they desire or feel they deserve. This is important not only in order to consider those individuals who have done better or worse than might be expected from the general situation, but to determine the extent to which various groups accept the criteria by which rewards came to be differentially allocated. It is to this question of expectations, and to the linked idea of salience, that we turn in the following chapter.

4 Orientations and Rewards

In this chapter we shall examine the various factors which operate to bring about differences in the orientations, that is the expectations and priorities, that people have in regard to the rewards available at work. We shall concentrate on four types of rewards – namely those relating to income, security, status, and intrinsic job. Unfortunately we could find no satisfactory way of dealing with social interaction. In addition we shall consider expectations with regard to promotion which, although it may be experienced as a reward in itself, is primarily important because it leads to increases in other rewards – though not, of course, always in all, even of the ones that we consider.

To begin with, however, we have to discuss two important issues relating to orientations and in particular to their two components: expectations and salience. These are firstly, what is the theoretical justification for dealing with orientations; and secondly, what is in fact meant by expectations and salience and, consequently, how have we set about trying to measure them? We do not here propose to discuss in any detail the concept of orientations as such, but to treat separately the two aspects of direct relevance to our analysis (for a fuller discussion of 'orientations' see Blackburn and Mann, 1979).

THE THEORETICAL ROLE OF EXPECTATIONS AND SALIENCE

There are two basic reasons for arguing the importance of orientations. The first is that there has been, quite rightly, a growing concern to offset the predominant emphasis in studies of industrial workers' behaviour on the homogeneity of individuals within the work situation. This disregard for the variable nature of individuals at work has been to a large extent a result of the influence exerted by the Human Relations School in this field. The initial reaction against them was prompted largely by a desire to demonstrate the variability of conditions within the employing organisation and so to argue the necessity of different, and in many cases conflicting, interests (see, for example, Scott *et al.*, 1956). However, this concern with internal differentiation, which was recognised by most of those involved as partial, itself came under criticism as evidence was presented to show that out-of-work experiences were significant factors in determining behaviour within the employment situation (see Zaleznik, Christensen Roethlisberger, 1958; Blauner, 1964 in his treatment of textile workers; Turner and Lawrence, 1965; Cunnison, 1966). This importance of non-work factors provides our second reason. In some cases the arguments have been linked with the advocacy of an 'action' approach (Goldthorpe, 1966;. Goldthorpe *et al.*, 1968; Silverman, 1968). For the most part this is unobjectionable, in so far as it directs attention to a particular set of possibly significant variables, the individual actor's perceptions and orientations. However the 'social action approach', with its emphasis on 'meaning', tends to stress interpretative understanding rather than causal explanation. For the former it is sufficient that the actor has a particular set of goals, or that a particular means to attain these goals can be seen by the observer to be, from the point of view of the actor, rational. Causal explanation, on the other hand, requires the construction of hypotheses relating goals or the choice of means to other factors. It becomes necessary to specify the conditions under which individuals will have particular goals, or will adopt a particular means to try to achieve their goals.

In practice, of course, many writers have seen the necessity of explaining goals, and not merely of assuming them as, for example, when Goldthorpe *et al.* (1968) relate an instrumental orientation to work to life-cycle effects. Equally, those who have demonstrated a relationship between factors of wider social background and behaviour or attitudes within the work situation, have felt the need to interpret such findings in terms of differences in individual orientations. However, scarcely anyone has attempted to tap these orientations directly, particularly in terms of both expectations and importance. It could be argued that there is no need to do so; if there are causal relationships between various wider social factors and orientations to work, and between the latter and behaviour or attitudes within the work situation, then we should be able to study the two relationships as one direct one without having to concern ourselves with psychological, motivational factors. Such an argument, however, ignores three important points, all of which are related to the question of theoretical adequacy. The first is that in the present state of sociological knowledge and theorising, we are unlikely to develop explanatory schemes which provide strong causal links between particular variables. Given the likely complexity of relationships between social factors and orientations, and between orientations and work behaviour, it is very probable that in trying to simplify, by relating the two sets of variables directly, we shall fail to provide an adequate explanation of work behaviour, because the relationships have become too attenuated. Even in the simplest case where two variables are each moderately strongly related to a third, intervening variable, the direct relationship will be fairly weak. Looking in a rather different way at what amounts to essentially the same point, it is through individuals' experience in the wider society that non-work factors influence their interpretation of work. Thus individuals are central to any theoretical explanation. They are central also to the process of data collection and our explanations will be better if we use all information available from this source.

The second point is also concerned with the question of the likely complexity of causal relationships that we have to deal with in this area. It may be that work behaviour is linked in other ways to wider social factors than through orientations, so the relevance of the latter needs testing. Considering solely the influence through orientations, it may operate not in the way hypothesised, but through aspects other than those we consider important.

So far, the word 'orientations' has been used rather vaguely, and we hope shortly to clarify our usage in this research. This vagueness, and the resultant lack of conceptual and theoretical clarity, can only be overcome, and this is our third point, by a clear statement of the relationships involving the various aspects of orientations, and such statements in turn should be empirically tested. Any attempt to deal directly with the relationships between work attitudes or behaviour and wider social factors is likely to be unsuccessful because of the complexity of the causal processes involved. It will also be unsatisfactory from a theoretical point of view, not only because an adequate theory should take account of the complexities, but also because any theory in this area is almost certain to make assumptions of some kind about orientations. Conceptual and theoretical clarity will only be attained if such assumptions are fully explored and elaborated. Finally, an adequate test of the theory will only be possible if this has been done.

Our task in this chapter is to deal with two aspects of orientations, which we refer to as expectations and salience. The general idea involved here is that various factors in earlier and current social experience generate in the individual expectations concerning the level of rewards that should accrue to him in the work situation, and priorities concerning these rewards relative to each other and to rewards outside the work situation. We regard these as two crucial, interconnected aspects (though perhaps not the only ones) of the way a worker relates to his work.

Expectations

The apparent simplicity of the idea of expectations in fact obscures their highly problematic nature, and the operationalisation of the idea is far from straightforward. The crucial problem lies in trying to distinguish empirically between what might be called 'wants' and our concept of expectations. Wants would refer to what individuals would want in some ideal sense, whereas expectations are what they realistically desire, given the situation in which they find themselves. The difficulty is that the idea of expectations clearly argues against individuals being too 'realistic', since if they were completely so they would expect precisely what they were in fact receiving. 'Reality', that is, would completely constrain their expectations, and perhaps even their wants as well. It is possible that in some situations this will occur, although the nature of wants even here remains problematic. Our conceptualisation of the latter is that they relate to an ideal situation, but because of this may have little relevance for actual behaviour. Of course, there may be conditions under which the ideal may be perceived to be more possible, and in this case wants and expectations become much more difficult to disentangle.

However, given that we are attempting to measure expectations rather than wants we are still left with some difficult problems. If individuals are not being completely 'realistic' in the sense suggested above, then their expectations will not perfectly match their actual rewards. In this case we would argue either that their wants are so strongly felt that they overcome the constraints of reality and come to be felt as needs, or that individuals develop a conception of due rewards and just deserts. Again this leads into the difficult area of the ideal and the actual, since we can distinguish between realistic notions of just rewards and more general value judgements. In the former case one can think of individuals as applying to themselves their perceptions of the generally accepted moral rules, while in the latter individuals would be basing their conceptions on a moral principle to which they adhere but, they may well be aware, others do not. The most obvious example of the first would be where it was a matter covered by law, but beyond this it clearly becomes difficult to determine the degree of acceptability of a moral rule and thus the extent to which the individual's conception of justice is realistic in the sense of the likelihood of it being accepted by others.

We can perhaps make this clearer, and illustrate some of the complexities, by considering two rewards, income and responsibility. Wants for the former may be regarded as unbounded in the sense that an increase is almost always considered desirable at any level. In practice, however, the ideal is not likely to be described as untold riches but as something more realistic (Patchen, 1968) in that it relates to conceivable improvement on the present. Expectations are more narrowly constrained and in a different way, as they are realistic in the sense that an individual's expected income is within the range that appears possible for someone like him. Shop-floor workers, for example, may have economistic orientations, but not expect to be paid as much as a senior manager. Responsibility, our other example, is not necessarily wanted and an increase may be viewed as a hardship in some cases. Wants, therefore, relate more to an optimal level than to maximisation. Thus wants are more attainable and so likely to be closer to expectations. However we should not overstate this, for responsibility is also a reward with a clear hierarchical distribution and the possibilities open to any individual, without making considerable sacrifices on other rewards, are severely constrained.

Moral evaluations relate to the realm of the possible, and although 'unrealistic' levels of reward are possible in principle and sometimes even in practice, they are rarely seen as such. Thus evaluations of just reward, which form expectations, are within the confines of the realistically possible as seen by the individual (Stewart and Blackburn, 1975). The two examples illustrate how these expectations are closer to present rewards than are wants. Being dependent on present position they are also likely to be in line with generally accepted principles, though this raises other complex issues.

It is clear that our knowledge of the relationships between wants and expectations, moral norms and moral imperatives, the ideal and the realistic is far from adequate. In particular, especially as concerns the present arguments, we do not know enough to enable us to be certain that we can tap those expectations – not entirely constrained by reality, based on not completely ideal conceptions of justice – which are relevant to the kinds of behaviour that we are considering. However, it is expectations in this sense that we have attempted to measure, although we would accept that under different conditions, or perhaps with reference to different kinds of behaviour, the expectations might be more or less constrained. In what follows we shall usually refer to expectations, but sometimes use the term desires as a reminder that what we have measured lies between the strictly realistic and the unconstrained ideal.

For the reasons discussed, the items that we have used in measuring expectations usually include the word 'ought' or 'should' rather than, say, 'like' or 'want'. Also, wherever possible we have made the item relate to the individual's job, rather than to the man himself. That is, we have tried to distinguish between those expectations that he holds as the incumbent of a particular position and those that he holds as an individual. Here again, the distinction is a difficult one empirically, but we think it necessary. Expectations which are held as an incumbent are those most likely to be significant for those aspects of behaviour which are related to the position. By dealing separately with expectations with regard to promotion we hoped to take account of those expectations which relate more to the individual as a person and to the possibility of his achieving higher rewards through a change in position, though the standard progressions through occupational careers severely limit the individual nature even of promotion.

Salience

One of the problems in the debate about orientations has been a failure to distinguish expectations regarding the level of rewards from the quite separate question of the importance of different rewards. In the Affluent Worker study (Goldthorpe *et al.*, 1968) for example, it is argued that car workers have an instrumental attitude to work, that is that they are more concerned with monetary than with other rewards. Whether or not this is the case, it should not be taken to mean that their expectations with regard to the level of monetary rewards are as high as those of, say, many professionals, who are usually taken to have a highly non-instrumental attitude to work. The problem of importance is less a matter of the level of a reward than of its significance to the individual, and one would expect that it would be a function not only of general social experience, but also of the extent to which the individual has achieved his expected level.

However, there has also been considerable ambiguity in the way that importance has been conceptualised. The apparently straight-forward request to respondents to indicate how important various rewards are to them in work is doubly unsatisfactory. In the first place it confuses the issue of what might be called general importance, that is the overall significance of work in providing for various needs, with what we shall refer to as salience, that is the extent to which, given the individual's current situation, a reward acts as an actual or potential motivating force for behaviour. The second confusion is linked both to the first and to the problem raised earlier, in respect of expectations, of the ideal versus the constrained and realistic. There is an implicit assumption that all rewards can be pursued on the basis of wants, in our terminology, and a failure to recognise that their availability is highly constrained. The voluntaristic assumption of the existence of free individual choice thus underlies both confusions, since by ignoring the second distinction it tends also to dissolve the first. This can be seen very clearly in Dubin's (1956) claim that work is not a 'central life interest' for most manual workers, because he finds that for the majority of them money is the most important reward from work. Clearly the most important reward, in the sense of that which is best satisfied in the actual situation of the present job, is not the same as the most important amongst all those desired (Kornhauser, 1965), nor as that which is most salient for action related to the job.

If the aim is to study general importance, the confusion may be to some extent reduced by trying to free respondents as far as possible from the constraints of their own present situation – by, for example, asking them to imagine that they are advising someone at the start of their working life. However, this will not do if, as in our case, the concern is with salience, for then one does not wish to abstract individuals from their present context but to get them to consider possible change within it. Salience thus is the extent to which an individual is motivated to pursue an improvement (or in some circumstances resist a deterioration) in a particular reward. Possibly the salience of a reward in this sense could be conceptualised as having an absolute value, but this would involve very great problems of measurement and of interpersonal comparison. Another approach, which is more tractable and potentially no less useful, is to consider salience as a relative phenomenon. By choosing a small number of, but nonetheless a comprehensive range of, rewards, one could determine the salience of each relative to the others; that is, given the situation in which the individuals find themselves, the extent to which they are concerned about each of the rewards available to them.

The relative salience of rewards

Our concern with importance, then, relates to the aspect of it that we have termed salience, and which we conceptualise as a question of relativities. Thus the measurement of the salience of all the rewards can be considered as a single process. In the next section we shall look at each separately when we also introduce expectations, but before this we can briefly examine the question of the measurement of salience and the relationships involved.

In our view the best way to determine relative salience was to ask the respondent to order the rewards in terms of the extent to which he would most want a small improvement in each. The inclusion of the word small was intended to indicate to the respondent that this was a question about marginal and hence possible improvements. It served also to ensure that the rewards would be reasonably commensurable, which they would cease to be if the question were to refer simply to improvements.

Our procedure was to present respondents with five cards, with written on each the phrase, 'in my job, I would welcome a small improvement in', followed by one of the following:

'income';
'the use and development of my abilities and aptitudes';
'security';
'contact with pleasant, interesting people';
'the respect that comes from doing a worthwhile, socially useful job'.

The cards were handed to the respondent after being shuffled, and he was asked to selected the one which represented the improvement he would most welcome, then the second, and so on.

The one of these which was most frequently placed first was use and development of abilities and aptitudes, that is intrinsic job rewards (unlike perceptions, we have included only this one aspect of intrinsic job rewards, which we regard as the more central). This accords with many other studies of the importance of various aspects of work for non-manual employees. However, it is followed very closely by income, and if we combine those who put each either first or second,

TABLE 4.1 *Salience of work rewards*

	Placing (%)					Correlations (Tau B)			
	First	*Second*	*Third*	*Fourth*	*Fifth*	*Intrinsic job*	*Income*	*Security*	*Status*
Intrinsic job	38.1	25.6	19.0	11.6	5.7				
Income	36.7	31.8	16.3	10.3	4.8	−0.33			
Security	10.7	14.1	17.1	21.5	36.6	−0.22	−0.07		
Status	9.8	15.7	24.9	27.2	22.5	−0.14	−0.15	−0.28	
Social interaction	4.7	12.4	22.7	29.4	30.8	−0.01	−0.15	−0.32	−0.19

NOTE: the percentage should sum to 100 both across rows and down columns, but there are small deviations because of the different Ns which result from incomplete responses in some cases.

the position is actually reversed. Comparatively few would most welcome an improvement in security, though times have changed and answers might be different now. Also less frequently chosen are respect from doing a worthwhile job, i.e. status, and contact with people, i.e. social interaction. The full distributions are shown in Table 4.1.

The results given in the table also allow us to say a little about the inter-relationships of the degrees of relative salience of the various rewards. All of the correlations are negative, since necessarily the choice of a particular rank for one reward prevents any other being ranked in the same position. However, those where giving greater importance to one reward tends to be more strongly associated with lesser importance to another are income with use of abilities, and security with social interaction, status or use of abilities.

DETERMINANTS OF ORIENTATIONS

In considering the influences shaping workers' priorities and expectations two different models are possible. The simpler one treats orientations as directly determined by background factors, and prior to the present work situation. Salience and expectations may also be seen as separately determined, without interaction, by the background factors. To take account of the individual's employment location and the rewards, perceptions, expectations and priorities that may derive from it calls for a more complex model. The general causal structure that we are assuming is the same in each of the following discussions, and it may be useful to outline it here. Diagrammatically it is shown in Figure 4.1, which should be straightforward. In this we take background factors first as having an influence on rewards and perceptions, as discussed in the previous chapter, and secondly as determinants of expectations. However, in considering expectations we also take account of actual rewards, or more precisely of the perceptions of them. We would hypothesise that the level of rewards currently experienced by the individual are likely to have a strong influence on his expectations. This is to be expected for wants in general, but even more so here, where we are dealing with realistic expectations. Thus, in considering the relationships of background factors to expectations we have to bear in mind their indirect influence through the attainment of a particular position and its associated level of rewards. Schooling beyond the minimum age, or qualifications, for

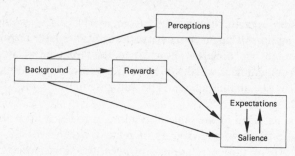

FIGURE 4.1   *Schematic representation of the structure of determinants of orientations*

example, may be related to the current level of expectations regarding, say, intrinsic job directly or only indirectly through their effect on occupational attainment. If there is no direct effect from the education variables this does not necessarily imply in any general sense that qualifications and so on have no influence on expectations. Rather it must be taken to mean that they have no direct influence at this time for the respondents in our sample, perhaps because for the great majority of them (who are all in non-manual occupations) their attainments have kept abreast of their expectations.

Structural factors and perceptions are potentially no less relevant to salience than to expectations. However, the situation is more complex, in that salience may be crucially related to the gap between expected and perceived rewards, both reflecting the discrepancy between what is desired and what is actually available. They do differ in two important respects though: firstly, salience is relative, in that the respondent is obliged to consider the desirability of an improvement in each reward as against the others; secondly, although there is a sense in which the salience of a reward must increase with the discrepancy, it is always possible for greater priority to be given to reducing a gap on one reward rather than a larger gap on another.

However, the relationship between the two measures means that we cannot assume any simple causal ordering between salience and expectations. That is we cannot easily say whether expectations regarding a particular reward are higher because that reward is important to the individual, or whether it is important to him because his expectations are higher, or rather, because the gap between his expectations and his achievements is greater. Our approach is to view both as necessarily arising out of the whole complex of circumstances in which the individual finds himself, including his various expectations and perceptions which interact with one another to constitute the relative salience of rewards. However at this stage, where we consider each reward singly, we shall not assume the causal priority of expectations.

The reason for dealing separately with each of the rewards is that to treat them together would be, at least in the first instance, unnecessarily complicated. Later on we shall be considering a more comprehensive model which includes relationships of orientations and perceptions of the different rewards.

Income

Ideally, one would like to be able to measure expectations simply by asking the individual about the level of rewards that he thinks that a man in his position ought to receive. There are two reasons why this is difficult. One concerns measurement problems which arise for some rewards, and we will return to it when we consider these. The other reason is that absolute levels in most cases have little meaning. This is so even in the case of income. The item we used here was: 'What would you say ought to be the average annual salary of a man of your age doing, broadly, your type of work?' Income has the advantage that it can be measured in easily understood, everyday units, but even here it is likely that the level of income expected for one's own job has little meaning when considered in isolation from the expected earnings of other groups. It is for this reason that we also asked respondents what they thought ought to be the incomes of 'an average manual worker' and 'an average top manager'. It will be appreciated that these questions on expectations correspond exactly to the questions on perceptions of actual incomes, with 'ought' replacing 'is', setting them within the same frames of reference. Again, following the pattern for perceptions, we distinguished in all cases between the situation within the establishment or company and in the community at large.

When we compare the estimates of the income of their own and other groups with their views on what these ought to be it seems that our respondents accept as justified the differentials between earnings within the company and outside for top managers and manual workers. Thus the average figure for what top managers in the company ought to earn is £4798, and for top managers outside it is £5127. The comparable figures for the annual earnings of manual workers are £1272 and £1248. The income which they believe people like themselves ought to earn in the company is £2009, and the comparable figure for those in the society is £2033. These amounts may be compared with what they see people as actually earning – £4227 and £4674, £1145 and £1109, and £1669 and £1733 respectively.

One thing that is immediately clear from these figures is that our respondents believe that all of the groups dealt with ought to be earning more than they are. Unfortunately we do not know whether this results simply from some kind of money illusion, or whether they do have in mind other groups whom they actually believe should be earning less. Even though our respondents believe that everyone, as far as we can tell, should be earning more, there are interesting differences in the proportionate increase that they seem, on average, to expect. The greatest proportionate increase they think desirable is 20 per cent, and that, unsurprisingly, is for their own group in the company. Similar people in the wider society are believed to deserve a slightly smaller increase of 17 per cent. Top managers within the company are also thought to warrant a greater increase than their counterparts outside (14 per cent as against 10 per cent). Manual workers, however, the only group who were seen as better-paid within the company than outside it, are also the only ones for whom the average increase thought desirable is lower for those in the respondent's company (11 per cent as against 13 per cent).

On average, respondents appear to be following two processes in deciding what the various groups ought to be paid. The first is one of improving the position of their most salient membership group, people doing similar jobs to themselves in the same firm, *vis-à-vis* all others. They would like virtually to eliminate the differential between themselves and similar people employed elsewhere. Within the company they want to increase their differential over manual workers (from 146 to 158 per cent) while at the same time reducing a top manager's differential over themselves (from 253 to 239 per cent).

The other process is one of equalisation as between earnings within their own company and in the wider society. This is best seen in relation to the differential between top managers and manual workers. The lower value for this is for perceived earnings in the company, and the higher for perceptions of incomes elsewhere. In moving to expectations of what each group ought to earn, the latter is reduced from 421 to 411 per cent, and the former increased from 369 to 377 per cent.

The outstanding feature of the determinants of expectations, in all cases, is the influence of the relevant perceptions (Table 4.2). The earnings each group is thought to have, whether in the company or in

TABLE 4.2 *Influence on expectations and salience of income (path coefficients)*

	Age	Father non-manual	Full-time further education	Part-time (evening) further education	Distance moved	Married	Owner-occupier	First job status	First job in firm status	Neighbours' status	Service in firm	Income	Extra income	Other household income	Present job status	Superiors: number	Own level, company	Own level, society	Manual worker, company	Manual worker, society	Top manager, company	Top manager, society	Residual
																	(Perceived income)						
Expectations																							
Own level																							
Company	—	—	—	—	0.02	—	—	-0.03	—	—	—	0.21	—	—	0.03	—	**0.29**	0.47	0.03	-0.02	—	—	0.31
Society	—	—	—	—	0.02	—	—	-0.03	—	—	—	0.22	0.02	—	0.03	—	—	**0.71**	—	—	—	—	0.38
Manual workers																							
Company	0.04	-0.03	—	—	—	—	-0.03	—	—	—	0.04	—	—	—	—	—	—	0.05	**0.64**	0.11	—	—	0.69
Society	0.08	—	—	0.03	—	0.06	-0.05	—	—	—	—	—	—	-0.04	—	0.05	—	—	0.15	**0.56**	—	—	0.75
Top manager																							
Company	—	—	—	—	0.03	0.04	—	—	-0.03	0.04	—	0.16	0.02	-0.02	—	—	0.09	0.05	—	—	**0.78**	0.10	0.47
Society	—	—	—	—	0.04	0.03	—	—	-0.03	0.03	—	—	—	—	—	—	—	—	—	—	0.06	**0.82**	0.47
Salience	-0.13	—	-0.05	-0.09	—	0.06	—	—	0.11	—	0.07	-0.17	—	—	—	—	-0.30	0.38	—	—	—	—	0.98

Paths from perceptions to corresponding expectations are shown in bold type.

society at large, is – with one interesting exception – the major determinant of the level of earnings that respondents believe that they ought to have. The exception is in the case of the respondent's own group in the company, where the strongest effect comes not from the perceived earnings in the company, but from those in society. This is a further indication of the process of social comparison referred to earlier, which leads to a belief in the group's right to a level of earnings commensurate with that of similar people in the wider society. Such comparisons are also made for manual workers and top managers, but in these cases the perceived level of earnings in the company remains more significant than that in society.

Few other factors make a direct contribution of any size to the level of earnings that respondents believe the various groups ought to have, either in the company or in the wider society. However, it is worth noting that those who are older tend to believe that manual workers ought to earn more.

Background factors are of some importance as determinants of the salience of income. Older respondents, and those with full-time or part-time evening education, give relatively less weight to an improvement in income; while those of longer service, those who are married and those who started in the firm in higher status positions tend to give it relatively more. Given that the other variables and present income have been controlled for, it seems probable that this last group is composed of those who have failed to keep up, in income terms, with their former colleagues.

More significant than any of the background factors are the effects that come from the individual's actual income and his perceptions of those of people like himself. As we would anticipate, those who earn more tend to place improvement in income lower in importance, but this effect is counteracted by its greater salience for those who think that similar people in the wider society have higher earnings. Here we have a further indication of the point made earlier about the significance of a reference group outside the individual's own employing establishment. It might have been expected that the comparison with people like themselves within the company would have a similar positive effect on salience. In fact the reverse is the case; not only is the influence in the same direction as that of his own income, but actually stronger. This suggests that respondents tend to identify with the occupational group, and it is this group, rather than the individual, which is seen as the major unit in the determination of income.

Status

Our strategy for dealing with expectations of status was similar and again matched the procedure for measuring perceptions. As before we made a distinction between the company and the wider society. Because there is no standard unit of measurement we adopted the same graphic approach, except that here we asked the respondent to indicate where he thought his job ought to be placed (with reference to 'prestige or social standing'). Scoring is again from 0 to 60 with manual workers and top managers scoring 5 and 55 respectively. A possible problem here is that the question asks the individual to say where he ought to be in an existing order, although he might wish to deny either the moral legitimacy or the empirical reality of that order, and so see himself as having no proper place in it. Such a radical view would also make the concept of expectations, as we are using it, rather inappropriate, since he would have no 'realistic' expectations. In practice, however, evaluations seem to have been far less revolutionary. A comparison may be made with the income questions, where respondents had the opportunity to evaluate the existing order, but rarely claimed that there ought to be anything more than quite modest changes.

When we compare the means of perceived and expected status, both in the community and in the company, we see again that perceptions and expectations are not widely discrepant (29.7 as against 32.8 in the community, and 28.7 as against 34.1 in the company). The discrepancy is greater in the latter case, because not only are perceptions lower but expectations are higher. However, this does not show up as clearly in the correlations where, if anything, actual and expected status are less well related in the community than in the company ($r = 0.69$ compared with $r = 0.72$). It is worth noting that the two expected status variables are more strongly related than the two perceived status ones ($r = 0.87$ as against $r = 0.71$), again an indication of a desire for greater consistency between the internal and the external situations.

If we now look at the determinants of expected status (Table 4.3) we find that the overwhelming influence in the case both of community and of company status is from the two perceptions. Desired status in each of these spheres is, naturally, determined most by the perception in the corresponding one, but there is also a substantial cross-effect from one sphere to the other. The perceptions are not the only influence on the expectations, but the remaining effects are quite small by comparison. It is clear that perceptions are critical intervening

TABLE 4.3 Influences on expectations and salience of status (path coefficients)

	Age	Qualifi-cations	Married	Income	Other house-hold income	Present job status	Subord-inates: number	Others: time	Company status	Society status	Residual
Expectations											
Company status	–	0.06	0.07	0.05	–	0.08	0.06	0.05	**0.44**	0.25	0.64
Society status	–	0.06	0.06	0.05	–	0.09	0.04	0.03	0.24	**0.44**	0.67
Salience	0.14	–	–	–	–0.05	–	–	–	–	–	0.99

Paths from perceptions to corresponding expectations are shown in bold type.

variables between background or structural factors and expectations.

One structural variable which has both an indirect and a direct effect is our measure of actual occupational status, which operates mainly through perceptions but also helps determine expectations directly. This is backed up by two other indicators of hierarchical position: income and the number of subordinates seen. Apart from level of qualifications and being married, there is very little evidence for any direct influence from background factors.

Finally, looking at influences on the salience of status, it is clear that the only one of importance is age. In addition there is some tendency for relative importance to be less the higher the amount brought in by other income-earners in the household.

Security

In the case of security we were faced with the dual problem of the lack of a unit of measurement and the strong elements of relativity. The only reasonable way of getting at expectations was through comparative questions. Thus we had to try to measure expectations of security using a graphical approach as with perceptions. The phrase 'Do you think your job ought to be . . . ?' was used to ask respondents to indicate their position in relation to five response points, ranging from 'much more secure' (22) to 'much less secure' (2). It will be recalled that in measuring perceptions of actual security the respondent was asked to compare his present position with those of a manual worker, a top manager and others doing his type of work. We cannot, therefore, relate expectations directly to perceptions. We might have attempted to match the approach for perceptions more closely and to obtain a measure of expectations or discrepancy relative to the security of others and thus independent of respondents' actual situations. However, this was not thought appropriate or practicable, primarily because it seemed unlikely that the questions entailed would hold much meaning for the respondents.

Clearly our measure in this case was not of expectations directly, but something which is a function of the perceived discrepancy between expectations and what is actually available. However, given that we had already measured perceptions, it did appear worth considering whether we had sufficient information to extract the expectations element of the gap. That is, if $G(ap) = E(xpectations) - P(erceptions)$, it seems to follow very simply that $E = G + P$. In practice matters are less simple, in that we have to make an assumption about the relationship of the perceptions as measured, P in the second equation, to those which are implicit, $(E+P)$ in the first equation. There is also the problem that there are three perceptions, so that some means of combining them must be found. Full details of the procedure adopted are given in Appendix II. Thus, it is important to bear in mind that although we start with the measurement of a 'gap', the variable subsequently referred to as 'expectations' is in fact a weighted combination of 'gap' and perceptions.

To look back at the gap, briefly, it is worth noting that on the whole there is no great expectation of more security – the average score is 14, just a little on the 'ought to be more secure' side of 'about the same'.

Turning now to the influences on expectations (Table 4.4) we see that the most significant feature is the importance of perceptions of security compared with a manual worker. Because of the way in which the measure of expectations was constructed, this reflects the fact that this comparison is more strongly correlated (negatively) with the individual's desired extra security than either of the others. The comparison with a top manager is much less important, and that with the individual's own group comparatively insignificant. The greater concern with non-membership groups is as we would expect, but that the comparison with manual workers should be so much more significant is interesting. Another point worth noting in regard to perceptions and expectations is that although the latter were obtained indirectly in this instance, the general level of influence of the former is very closely comparable with that in the case of status. This suggests that the assumptions made in constructing the variable were reasonable ones.

Apart from these three perceptions the only effects to note are that older respondents and those with more dependents have higher expectations, as also do those who see more subordinates. Expectations tend to be lower for those with higher-status friends and the better-qualified.

When we turn to salience we find that here, too, it is the comparisons with other groups which are most significant. Again the effect is very much more marked where the comparison is with manual workers than when it is with top managers. However, the influence is now in the opposite direction – the more secure the individual considers himself as compared with either group, the less relative importance he gives to an improvement in security.

Other variables, interestingly, operate in the same direction as they do with expectations. That is, older respondents – but surprisingly not

TABLE 4.4 *Influences on expectations and salience of security (path coefficients)*

	Age	Qualif- ications	Number of dependents	Friends' status	Neighbours' status	Subordinates Time	Subordinates Number	Superiors: time	Others Time	Others Number	Security Own level	Security Manual worker	Security Top manager	Residual
Expectations	0.09	-0.06	–	-0.08	–	–	0.06	–	–	–	0.09	0.48	0.27	0.75
Salience	0.10	-0.07	-0.05	-0.07	0.06	0.09	–	0.05	-0.06	0.07	–	-0.22	-0.10	0.91

those with more family responsibilities – place greater emphasis on security, while the better qualified and those with higher-status friends, and in this case also neighbours, place less. Social interaction at work has rather more influence on salience, with positive effects from the time spent with subordinates and superiors, and the number of colleagues seen, but an opposite effect from time spent with colleagues.

Intrinsic job

The problem of relativity in the units of measurement occurred most sharply in the case of expectations regarding intrinsic job rewards, and here we were unable to be as explicit in providing comparisons as we were elsewhere. In this instance our approach was somewhat different, and we used a number of Likert-type items with five response categories. The difficulties here are similar to those entailed in measuring perceptions of intrinsic rewards, and the strategy is essentially the same. Four items were used in the final scale, constructed by means of factor analysis, and loadings are shown below. It is clear that the second item contributes more to the composite than any other.

> 'I should be happier if I had more responsibility' (0.55).
> 'I should like to be able to use more of my own ideas on this job' (0.72).
> 'The company ought to do more to allow people to increase their knowledge and abilities' (0.53).
> 'My job ought to be much more varied than it is' (0.58).

Since expectations regarding intrinsic job rewards are a composite, in considering their level it is probably easier to consider the individual items which were scored on the basis of five response categories ranging from strongly agree to strongly disagree. The highest degree of agreement is with the item relating to more responsibility, followed by those concerned with the use of more of the respondent's own ideas, and the company doing more to allow people to increase their knowledge and abilities. On the other hand, there is a slight tendency to disagree with the item suggesting the job should be much more varied than it is.

The variable constructed from these items is similar to the initial measure of security in that it relates to a discrepancy between per-

TABLE 4.5 *Influences on expectations and salience of intrinsic job rewards (path coefficients)*

	Age	Father non-manual	Years at school	Part-time (evening) further education	Distance moved	Number of moves	Married	Income	Other house-hold income	Friends' status	Attendance at political associations	Others: time	Use of abilities	Control	Residual
Expectations	−0.16	0.04	–	0.04	0.06	–	0.08	–	0.05	–	0.04	0.05	0.42	0.24	0.81
Salience	−0.26	–	0.08	0.08	–	0.05	–	0.12	–	0.08	–	–	−0.10	–	0.95

ceptions and expectations rather than to the latter directly. We have therefore used the same procedure to derive a measure of expectations from the gap and the direct measures of perceptions (see Appendix II for details).

It is rewards, or rather the perceptions of them, which are by far the most important determinants of expectations (Table 4.5). Although given the nature of the measure this is not very surprising, it is reassuring that as with security the coefficients are of a similar order of magnitude to those relating to status. Of the two perceptions, use of abilities has a far stronger effect than control. The only other variable that has a strong influence is age, with older respondents expecting less. As we saw in the previous chapter, there is some tendency for age to be associated with lower perceptions of use of abilities. Since we are measuring the direct effect, after the effects of other variables have been partialled out, we can be fairly sure that older respondents do genuinely have lower expectations. We would suggest that this reflects realistic adaptation to the situation. With this exception we can again see that background factors act primarily through the intervening perceptions of rewards.

There is support for the explanation proposed for the effect of age on expectations when we look at the salience of intrinsic job rewards. This factor has by far the most important influence in reducing salience, considerably more than the only perception which is significant, that is use of abilities. The reduction in salience is a clear indication that with experience intrinsic job rewards are no longer sought to the same extent in work.

All of the other significant factors serve to increase the salience. Two are educational variables, even though these appear to be of little importance in the case of expectations. They are years at school beyond the minimum and time spent in part-time evening education. Geographical mobility too is of some significance, in this case as measured by the number of moves. There are two other effects. One is from the status of the respondent's friends and the other from income. The latter (and to some extent the former) lends some support to the argument that as rewards of a certain kind increase, so the importance of other rewards becomes greater. We shall return to this point later.

Social interaction

Neither of the last two rewards that we consider can be dealt with as

TABLE 4.6 *Influences on salience of social interaction (path coefficients)*

Age	Married	Number of dependents	First job status	Neighbours' status	Others		Social interaction perceptions	Residual
					Time	*Number*		
0.10	−0.09	−0.06	0.07	0.07	0.08	−0.06	−0.10	0.98

fully as the previous ones. In the case of social interaction we could devise no satisfactory measure of expectations, and we must therefore leave that aspect. However, we can consider the salience of social interaction rewards which, it may be remembered, were least often chosen as being the ones where an improvement would be most welcome (Table 4.6).

Two of the factors which lead people to assign lesser importance to social interaction are directly related to this aspect of work. One is the number of co-workers that are seen in a normal working day and the other is the measure of perceptions. The remaining two are concerned with family relationships, both being married and having more dependents.

Greater relative importance is assigned to social interaction rewards primarily by those who are older and by those whose first job was, or whose neighbours are, of higher status. The effect of the number of co-workers seen is also largely offset by the time actually spent with them. Apparently, meeting more colleagues leads to greater social interaction rewards and a consequent lessening of their salience, but spending more time with them has the opposite effect.

Promotion

Finally we come to the question of the individual and his personal advancement. This aspect was thought to be unsuitable for inclusion in the measure of relative salience. It is also the one where the problems of conceptualisation and measurement of expectations were probably greatest of all. To some extent it was possible to follow a procedure similar to the one adopted for intrinsic job rewards, and to use items relating to the discrepancy between the available and the desirable. However, the single item of this kind that we included – 'This job ought to provide much better opportunities for getting ahead' – seemed to cover this aspect well, and in any event it seemed preferable to try to tap the expected as directly as possible. Measures that had previously been used for achievement motivation did this as well as we could anticipate, especially those that dealt with the evaluation of promotion as against other values (Seeman, 1958; see also Neal and Rettig, 1963). Thus we used the following Likert-type items with the factor loadings shown. It is worth noting that the negative loading of the third item suggests emphasis on promotion is associated with short- or medium-term financial returns.

(1) 'I would not let friendship ties stand in the way of moving on to a better job' (0.32).
(2) 'I prefer a steady job to taking a chance on one that might lead to promotion' (−0.69).
(3) 'I would rather take a job with long-term prospects than one paying a high salary' (−0.31).
(4) 'I wouldn't take a promotion, no matter how big an improvement it was for me, if it meant that I might endanger my health' (−0.41).
(5) 'I really prefer to put my roots down somewhere, rather than move as the chances for advancement come along' (−0.68).

Of these items most agreement is shown with the first. However, second-highest agreement is with one of the items with a negative weighting, indicating less concern with promotion than with a possible danger to health. There is somewhat lower agreement by respondents that long-term considerations are to be given preference over more immediate returns; and general disagreement with the remaining two items. Finally, there is the one item that was previously referred to and that was used on its own: 'This job ought to provide much better opportunities for getting ahead'. Here again there was moderate agreement on average.

This last item relates more to the gap between expectations and perceptions, but attempts to modify it in the same way as with intrinsic job and security were unsuccessful. As we would expect, those who have a favourable view of their promotion opportunities are very much less likely to express agreement with the statement that their job should provide more (Table 4.7). Given this we might also anticipate a similar result for the specific case of opportunities outside the individual's present firm. In fact the reverse is the case; a clear indication that this is a cause of dissatisfaction with the organisation, which is being compared unfavourably with others. Thus, those who see good opportunities outside are more likely to believe that their present job should provide better. Not surprisingly, also, even allowing for the fact that the influence of perceptions is being controlled for, those with higher incomes are less likely to agree with the statement.

Those who have come from larger communities of origin, and those who have moved further, believe that they should have better opportunities, while there is a negative effect from the status of the res-

TABLE 4.7 *Influences on expectations of promotion (path coefficients)*

	Age	Community of origin	Father's status	Qualifications	Distance moved	Number of moves	First job status	Service in firm	Income	'Opportunities outside'	Promotion perceptions	Residual
'Better opportunities'	–	0.06	–	–	0.06	–	–0.06	–	–0.11	0.12	–0.47	0.86
Expectations	–0.26	–	0.12	–0.05	–	0.06	–	–0.07	0.17	0.08	–	0.93

pondent's first job. This last is in accordance with what might have been expected, which is that those who started in lower positions would tend to have a more favourable view of the promotion opportunities within the firm. However the effect is slight, and in any case was not apparent when perceptions themselves were considered. It is possible that we have here a mixture of those individuals still in lower positions, who have less favourable opinions, and those who may have moved upwards, whose opinions would be more favourable.

A striking feature of Table 4.7 is that the factors influencing the two measures are highly dissimilar, reflecting the different natures of the measures. This may be seen most clearly with regard to perceptions of promotion prospects, where the large negative influence on the belief that opportunities should be better disappears entirely for the second measure; the worse they think their prospects are the more they want them improved, but there is no effect on the views of what level they ought to be.

Age, on the other hand, shows the opposite pattern. Thus for the more general measure it is the single most important influence, and there is in addition a smaller, also negative, effect from length of service in the firm. Even though this variable is somewhat like achievement motivation, the items that go to make it up are concerned with potential decisions about taking a different job. Older, and longer-service persons are clearly less likely to value prospects of advancement and to place more emphasis on security in their present position.

Whereas those with higher earnings tended to disagree that their job should provide better opportunities for promotion, they are more likely to have higher expectations of promotion in the more general sense. Further evidence for regarding this aspect of expectations as a basic one comes also from the influences from background variables. One of the mobility measures, the number of moves, has some effect but rather greater, and demonstrating the importance of socialisation or perhaps of reference groups, is that from father's occupational status. These results illustrate the importance of using measures of the level of expectations rather than depending on 'gap' measures.

At this point a brief word on the two possible models of influences on orientations which we mentioned earlier will be useful. We have presented the more complex model but we also tested the simpler one which treats orientations as prior to the work situation and directly determined by background factors. The model presented incorporating rewards and perceptions as intervening variables proved much more useful, particularly for expectations. This may be seen most clearly in the increases in the squared multiple correlation coefficients, which provide estimates of the improvement in the proportion of variance explained. In the case of expectations these are considerable; for example from 41 to 91 per cent for earnings of the respondent's own group in the company, from 16 to 55 per cent for status in society, from 1 to 44 per cent for security and from 7 to 34 per cent for intrinsic job rewards. Only for promotion – a rather different sort of reward – was there no clear evidence of improvement (only an increase from 10 to 13 per cent). The models were generally less successful in explaining salience, and any improvements with the more complex model were small, the most marked being from 8 to 17 per cent for security. However, overall there can be no doubt that the fuller model adds significantly to our understanding of the determinants of orientations.

Inter-relationships of expectations and perceptions

So far we have considered the expectations and perceptions of each of the rewards separately. However two questions naturally arise. As we saw in the previous chapter, perceptions of the different rewards vary positively together, and it is therefore interesting to see whether this fact has consequences for expectations. Table 4.8 suggests that it has, in that the latter also are in general positively related to one another. The strongest inter-relationships are those among income, status and intrinsic job expectations. The other two, security and promotion, which provide the only instance of a negative correlation (albeit a small one), are also well related to status and intrinsic job respectively. The fact that the relationships involving security and intrinsic job are comparable with the remainder is further evidence of the satisfactory nature of these constructed measures.

The second question that arises is whether the perceptions of one reward have any influence on the expectations of some other reward. The question derives in part from the possibility that a greater amount of one reward may lead the individual to expect less of another. So, for example, we might find that someone who earns more expects to have less of intrinsic job rewards in his work, or at least has lower levels of desired use of abilities and control. Alternatively one could argue that, given the generally hierarchical nature of the overall reward distribution, those with higher income are likely to expect a higher level of intrinsic job rewards. Similar arguments apply to

TABLE 4.8   *Inter-relationships of expectations (correlation coefficients)*

	Income, own level	Company status	Security	Intrinsic job
Company status	0.51			
Security	0.14	0.23		
Intrinsic job	0.25	0.33	0.16	
Promotion	0.11	0.15	−0.07	0.25

salience also. To an extent by including income and occupational status in all the analyses, we have already dealt with this. However, we can now consider it more fully.

Table 4.9 shows the results of the combined analysis in which perceptions of each reward were allowed to influence expectations of all rewards. Since the effects of background and structural variables were similar to those noted earlier in the individual analyses they have, for the sake of clarity, been mostly omitted from the table. In fact the two types of analysis are also similar in showing the considerable importance of the perceptions of a particular reward in the corresponding expectations.

The most valuable result from the combined analysis is the evidence for the importance of perceptions of promotion. Viewing promotion as a strategy leads us to expect that those individuals with a more favourable view of their prospects would place less emphasis on immediate returns in their present job. As may be seen from the table this is correct; perceptions of promotion do have a negative influence on the expectations regarding all other rewards, most particularly intrinsic job and status in the company. That is, those who believe that the promotion prospects within their company are better tend to expect lower intrinsic job rewards and a lower level of security, and are less likely to believe that their present status in the company should be higher or even that people like themselves in the company should earn more. It must be kept in mind that expectations relate to the present situation, and are not of future rewards allowing for a realistic view of promotion chances.

However, this effect comes only from perceptions of promotion within the organisation. In two cases those who see good opportunities outside have higher rather than lower expectations. This is so for company status and intrinsic job. It is thus not generalised ideas about promotion prospects which are significant, but those that

TABLE 4.9 *Influences of perceptions on expectations: combined analysis (path coefficients)*

Expectations	Perceived incomes									Security:							Residual
	Income	Own level, company	Own level, society	Manual worker, company	Top manager, company	Present job status	Company status	Society status	Use of abilities	Control	Own level	Manual worker	Top manager	Promotion	'Opportunities outside'	Superior	
Income	0.19	0.31	0.44	0.02	—	0.03	—	—	0.03	—	0.02	—	—	-0.04	—	—	0.30
Company status	—	—	0.08	—	-0.05	0.09	0.44	0.24	0.06	—	—	—	—	-0.08	0.08	—	0.63
Intrinsic job	—	—	—	—	—	—	—	—	0.48	0.26	—	—	—	-0.13	0.12	-0.09	0.79
Security	—	0.18	—	0.07	-0.06	—	—	—	—	—	-0.08	0.48	0.28	-0.04	—	—	0.75
Promotion	—	—	—	—	—	—	—	0.07	—	—	—	—	—	—	0.07	—	0.92
'Better opportunities'	—	—	—	—	—	—	-0.10	—	—	—	—	—	-0.05	-0.46	0.11	—	0.86

are offered, in a way similar to other rewards, by the individual's present job with his current employer.

No other variable has quite so important an effect as does the perception of promotion prospects, but some others stand out. Promotion expectations themselves tend to be greater, the higher the individual's perceptions of the earnings of his own group in the company, and less the more he thinks that top managers earn.

One of the intrinsic job variables, use of abilities, has a positive influence on expectations of status in the company, which are also affected by perceptions of the earnings of the individual's occupational group in the society. This latter is interesting because it replaces the direct effect seen earlier from the respondent's actual earnings. Thus, in so far as the level of status thought desirable is influenced by income, it is that of the occupation generally in the community.

What stands out, then, from this examination of the effects of perceptions of the various rewards upon the expectations of other rewards, is firstly the important influence of promotion perceptions which, in all cases, serve to reduce expectations with respect to other rewards. Secondly we should note that the general tendency elsewhere is for higher perceptions of one reward to increase expectations with respect to another, though nowhere is the effect very marked.

When we turn to a similar examination of salience the results are for the most part little different from those presented previously. There are a few additional influences, the most notable ones being from perceptions of security, especially the comparison with an average manual worker. We have already noted that it is this comparison which is the most important for reducing the salience of security. Now we find also that the more favourably the individual compares himself with a manual worker, the greater is the relative salience of status ($p = 0.10$), social interaction ($p = 0.08$) and income ($p = 0.06$). For the first two of these there is also a positive influence from the respondent's view of his own security as compared with an average top manager ($p = 0.07$ in both cases). The only other important changes involve perceptions of social interaction. The more favourable these are, the greater the salience of security ($p = 0.08$) and income ($p = 0.06$), but the lower that of intrinsic job ($p = -0.05$).

Although we argued earlier that it is difficult to establish any causal ordering between expectations and relative salience, that is whether expectations are raised because a particular reward is more important or whether it becomes important because of higher expectations, it is nonetheless interesting to consider a model which makes the assumption that expectations determine importance. Among other things this enables us to show clearly the asymmetric effects of perceptions and expectations upon salience, as well as giving some indication of the relationships between different rewards.

The asymmetry of perceptions and expectations shows up most clearly in the case of income (Table 4.10). Thus, the higher the individual's actual earnings and the more he believes that people like himself in the company do earn the less salient to him is income. However, salience is greater the more he believes that people like himself should earn. There is a similar pattern with the salience of both security and intrinsic job (there is no measure of social interaction expectations) although in these cases there is an element of artificiality given the way the expectations were measured. It is nevertheless of interest that in the case of security we still find that the greatest effect is from the comparison with a manual worker. The pattern is less marked with intrinsic job rewards. Here, in line with our earlier findings, the main contribution is from use of his abilities rather than perceptions of control, both serving to reduce salience.

Certain of these opposing influences also operate on the salience of other rewards. Higher earnings tend to increase the salience of intrinsic job rewards, but it is lowered by a higher level of expected earnings. Similarly greater security (when compared with a manual worker) makes an increase in these rewards more important; greater desired security makes it less. In fact perceptions and expectations of security operate in a similar way upon the salience of social interaction and of status. Finally, although not as pronounced as in the opposite direction, there is a tendency for those whose jobs use more of their abilities and which give them more control to place more emphasis on income, countered by a lower emphasis where intrinsic job expectations are higher.

Interestingly, no such phenomenon is found involving promotion. In fact perceptions of promotion opportunities appear to have no influence at all on the relative importance of other rewards. On the other hand expectations of promotion do. In particular those with higher expectations give greater weight to an increase in intrinsic job rewards and less weight to increases in either security or social interaction.

Looking back over both expectations and salience together, although there is general evidence that the different rewards are related, in such a way that increases in some lead to a greater emphasis on others, it is impossible to point to any simple relationship, such as a

TABLE 4.10 *Influence of perceptions and expectations on salience of rewards (path coefficients)*

| | Income | Own level earnings | Security: | | | Use of abilities | Control | Social interaction perceptions | Superior perceptions | Ought own level income | Security expectations | Intrinsic job expectations | Promotion expectations | Residuals |
			Manual worker	Top manager	Own level									
Income	−0.27	−0.42	0.05	–	–	0.07	0.06	–	–	0.63	–	−0.12	–	0.96
Status	–	–	0.16	0.10	–	0.07	–	–	0.05	–	−0.12	–	–	0.97
Security	–	–	−0.39	−0.19	−0.07	0.05	0.07	0.08	0.06	–	0.31	–	−0.13	0.86
Intrinsic job	0.32	0.19	0.09	–	–	−0.19	−0.08	–	–	−0.26	−0.10	0.23	0.13	0.91
Social interaction	–	–	0.13	0.11	–	–	–	−0.10	–	–	−0.10	−0.05	−0.07	0.98

* The results presented are those when other factors are also included in the analysis.

progressive ordering of rewards. While we find, for example, that those earning more tend to place more emphasis on an improvement in the way their job uses their abilities, we find also that those who see their jobs as providing them with more control and use of their abilities give greater weight to improvements in income. It is of course possible that a more detailed analysis might reveal a pattern, especially if it involved a consideration of development over time, but none is indicated by our results.

Considering this section as a whole there can be no doubt that systemic factors, and in particular the associated rewards and perceptions, play an important part in the explanation of orientations. This means that it is misleading to think of *prior* orientations. To do so entails an artificial division between work and non-work life which is not supported by the evidence. Orientations to work are not just something brought into work from outside; they derive from an individual's total experience. Background factors certainly have an influence here, but we have seen that present work experience is of crucial importance in shaping these orientations. Once this is allowed for the continuing direct effects from social background are very limited. The main exception to this is age, which has quite a marked effect on the salience of all five rewards, decreasing that of income and use of abilities, and increasing that of security, status and social interaction. As far as security and intrinsic job are concerned this is reflected in expectations, and it is also clear that older workers have much lower expectations regarding promotion.

While this last is scarcely surprising, it is worth commenting on some of the other results. Again the greater salience of security for older workers is quite comprehensible, but it should be noted that the lower salience of income goes together with relatively high expectations. As we saw in the previous chapter, as they get older non-manual workers tend to progress to better-paid jobs, but this progression is matched by expectations. On the other hand, older workers in our sample experience lower intrinsic job rewards, taking into account factors such as income which are related to this progression, and this is accompanied by even lower expectations. This illustrates the importance of not confusing employment location, which is related to age, at a point of time, with patterns of individual change over time.

These results point up the way in which the relationship between expectations and salience, which is generally positive, is made more complex by the effect of other variables. Thus both income and intrinsic job rewards decline in relative importance for older respondents, while the level of expectations of the two rewards actually rises. Again, although both status and security are more salient for older employees, this is only reflected in their levels of expectations. This demonstrates the validity of an approach which treats expectations and salience as distinct, examining the complementary way in which both arise out of the relation between social background, structural location and experience of rewards.

One point that has emerged clearly in our analysis is the importance of the individual's perceptions of his chances of promotion for his expectations of other rewards. Promotion is one of the major means by which a presently undesirable situation may be avoided, and it would appear that even its undesirability may be lessened if the individual sees good prospects for advancement. In the following chapter we shall consider first, satisfaction, and then the various ways other than promotion by which the individual's position may be accommodated or improved.

5 Work Satisfaction and Individual Adaptation

Having in the previous chapters considered the processes by which individuals come to be located in the structure of reward distribution, and the perceptions and expectations that they have regarding rewards, we are now ready to turn to the question of their reactions to their situation. We begin by looking at the degrees of satisfaction expressed with the various work rewards, assessing the relationship to these of social background, perceptions and expectations, and salience. Subsequently we shall consider the significance of satisfaction for ways of adapting to the employment situation. For the present we shall consider only those ways that primarily concern individuals, leaving until the following chapter the question of collective responses.

SATISFACTION

Information on the extent of each respondent's satisfaction with the rewards that we have previously discussed was gathered by presenting him with a line marked in small segments, and above it verbal descriptions, ranging from 'more or less completely satisfied' (scored 52), through 'very satisfied' (44), 'fairly satisfied' (36), to 'half and half' (28), and similarly through to 'more or less completely dissatisfied' (4). Responses were scored simply by measuring along the line from the 'dissatisfied' end, giving a range from 0 to 56. On each reward the average score represents a degree of satisfaction rather than dissatisfaction, which is in line with the usual findings on job satisfaction. The lowest mean score is with income (29) and the next lowest with promotion (31). Following these are satisfaction with status (34), intrinsic job (37), immediate superior (38), social interaction (39) and security (40). The last four of these fall well within the range of the 'fairly satisfied' response.

114

It is interesting to draw a comparison here with the results from a sample of manual workers. In their case satisfaction with security and promotion was lower, the latter coming well below income, leaving social interaction as clearly the highest source of satisfaction (Blackburn and Mann, 1979, 169). The differences are in accord with the actual rewards in that the white-collar workers do enjoy greater promotion prospects and security, but by the same token we might have expected greater satisfaction with pay and intrinsic job rewards. This illustrates the importance of taking into account levels of expectations as well as actual rewards.

When we compare our results with those obtained earlier in looking at the relative importance of the five rewards, there are some interesting differences. For the most part the two sets of results are consistent with one another, in the sense that high importance goes with low satisfaction. The relatively low degree of satisfaction with income reflects the high importance attached to this factor and at the other extreme, the relatively high satisfaction with security and with social interaction reflects the low importance of security and people. The two discrepant cases are intrinsic job, which is second most important despite the fact that satisfaction is relatively high, and status which, although satisfaction is a little lower, is quite a long way behind in terms of importance.

These results should alert us to the problems involved in talking about satisfaction, a point to which we shall return shortly. Expressed satisfaction with some aspect of the job and the desire for change or the likelihood of behaviour to bring about change in that reward, are not necessarily directly related. As we can see in the case of intrinsic job rewards, there may be relatively high satisfaction and yet a relatively strong emphasis on an increase in this kind of reward. Conversely, as in the case of status, satisfaction may be comparatively low, but improvements on this factor may be of no great importance to most individuals.

We have seen in the previous two chapters that both the perceptions and the expectations of different rewards are fairly well inter-correlated. Thus we would expect the various satisfactions also to be quite well related to one another, and in fact this is the case. The strongest relationships are between status, intrinsic job and promotion followed by those between social interaction, superior and intrinsic job, and income, status and promotion. One way of summarising the whole set of inter-relationships is to look at the multiple correlation between each satisfaction measure and all of the others. If we do this, we find that satisfaction with intrinsic job is best related to the remainder (R = 0.64), followed by satisfaction with status (R = 0.62), and with promotion (R = 0.60). The least related is satisfaction with security (R = 0.40). Intermediate are satisfaction with income (R = 0.52), with immediate superior (R = 0.56) and with social interaction (R = 0.57). Much the same results are found if we adopt another approach to the same question, that is by carrying out a factor analysis of the correlations. When this is done we find that there is only one significant factor (i.e. with an associated eigenvalue greater than one) accounting for some 45 per cent of the original variance. The loadings of each of the satisfaction measures on this single factor parallel the multiple correlations very closely. Thus the three with the highest loadings are intrinsic job (0.75), status (0.67) and promotion (0.65), and those with the lowest are security (0.44) and income (0.53).

We have argued earlier that satisfaction with any aspect of the individual's job is primarily a function of expectations with regard to a particular reward, and perceptions of the level of that reward being achieved. How far this is so, and to what extent other factors continue to have a direct effect on satisfaction, we shall investigate shortly. Before then we must consider what we mean by satisfaction with some aspect of the job. The problems involved here are related to those discussed earlier in considering the nature of expectations. The difficulty in the latter case was that these could vary between the individual's ideal situation, on the one hand, and that constrained by the immediate reality on the other. If we accept expectations as a factor determining satisfaction, then there is a similar problem as to which aspect of expectations is being taken into account by individuals when they express a degree of satisfaction or dissatisfaction.

Individuals make a number of decisions concerning their jobs: whether to look around for another, actually to move to another job, or perhaps to join a trade union. All these may be regarded as depending on satisfaction with the job, but individuals are much less likely to be clear on what is wanted when they are asked about their satisfaction. For most people this is a contrived question, and not one that they ask themselves in quite this way in everyday life. In answering it they must take account of what the job provides as against what they think it ought to provide. There is a good deal of evidence from other studies that in this latter part many people are highly constrained by their immediate situation, and so their expressions of satisfaction are not at all to be taken as expressions of happiness or pleasure in that situation. Rather that, all things considered, they are satisfied only in the sense that they could not be faring much better. Where questions are used which, to a greater extent, free them from their immediate constraints, then 'satisfaction' appears to be much less. We shall be able to look to this point again later on, when we consider actual or potential behaviour as related to expressions of satisfaction.

Determinants of satisfaction

Let us begin by looking at the determinants of satisfaction with each of the rewards excluding expectations and perceptions (Table 5.1). The relatively strong influence of income, in all but two of the seven cases, is the outstanding feature of the table. Otherwise, few general points emerge, except perhaps the influence of age on satisfaction with intrinsic job and superior, and the apparent significance of the time spent with superiors, or the number of colleagues and subordinates seen.

In moving on to consider a model which includes both perceptions and expectations we have allowed for all of these to operate upon each of the satisfactions. We shall deal a little later with some of the cross-effects that result from this, but for the present the main point to note is the very clear pattern in which for each reward, satisfaction is increased by more favourable perceptions, and decreased by higher expectations (except where we have no expectation measures for the two social interaction variables). The magnitude of these opposing effects varies but it is again worth noting that the results for the two constructed expectations, security and intrinsic job, are not out of line with the remainder (Table 5.2).

In the case of income, the high inter-correlations between some of the variables probably exaggerate the pattern, but one interesting point emerges thereby. This is the significance of the individual's own occupational group. As we have noted before, the individual identifies with his own group in the company, so here we find strong opposing effects. On the other hand he compares himself with the same group in the wider society; thus the more they are seen as earning, the lower the degree of satisfaction. Neither of the other reference groups appears to be important, however, whereas with security it is again the comparison with manual workers which has the strongest influence.

One or two other points are worth noting because they also provide further demonstration of earlier findings. In particular, the fact that satisfaction with promotion prospects is not significantly affected by

TABLE 5.1   *Influences on satisfactions: background and situational factors only (path coefficients)*

Satisfaction	Age	Father in union	Type of school	Further education			Distance moved	Married	Owner-occupier	Income	Other household income	Friends' status	Neighbours' status	Superiors: time	Subordinates: number	Others: number	Residual
				Full-time	Part-time (day)	Part-time (evening)											
Income	—	—	—	—	-0.06	—	—	—	-0.05	0.33	—	-0.08	—	0.05	—	—	0.95
Security	—	—	0.06	—	—	—	—	—	—	—	—	0.09	0.08	—	—	—	0.98
Status	0.05	-0.06	-0.05	—	—	—	-0.05	—	—	0.23	—	—	—	—	0.05	—	0.96
Intrinsic job	0.12	-0.06	—	-0.07	—	-0.05	—	0.07	—	0.17	—	—	—	0.07	0.06	0.06	0.95
Superior	0.11	—	—	—	—	—	—	—	—	—	—	—	—	0.16	—	—	0.98
Social interaction	—	—	—	—	—	-0.06	—	—	—	0.14	—	—	—	0.09	—	0.07	0.99
Promotion	—	—	—	—	—	—	—	—	—	0.12	-0.06	—	—	0.05	0.13	0.07	0.98

TABLE 5.2 *Influences on satisfactions: corrected analy...*

Perceptions

Satisfaction	Age	Type of school	Full-time further education	Married	Owner-occupier	Friends' status	Service in firm	Income	Present job status	Others: number	Own-level income: Company	Own-level income: Society	Own level	Manual worker	Top manager	Company status	Society status	Use of abilities	Control	Superior	Social interaction	Promotion	'Opportunities outside'
Income	—	−0.05	—	—	—	—	—	0.53	—	—	0.70	−0.22	0.06	—	—	0.11	—	0.10	—	0.08	—	0.20	−0.08
Security	0.06	—	—	—	—	—	—	—	−0.06	—	—	—	0.19	0.54	0.26	0.32	—	0.08	0.08	0.08	—	0.07	—
Status	0.11	−0.06	—	—	−0.05	−0.05	−0.05	−0.26	—	—	0.25	—	0.05	—	—	0.07	0.16	0.13	0.24	0.06	0.06	0.13	—
Intrinsic job	0.14	—	−0.06	—	—	—	−0.05	—	—	—	0.22	−0.05	0.06	—	—	—	—	0.38	0.05	0.10	0.10	0.09	—
Superior	—	—	—	—	—	—	—	—	—	—	—	—	—	—	—	—	—	0.07	—	0.72	0.04	—	—
Social interaction	—	—	—	−0.05	—	—	—	—	—	0.06	—	—	—	—	—	—	—	0.10	0.08	0.15	0.42	0.07	—
Promotion	—	—	—	—	—	—	—	—	−0.05	—	—	—	0.03	—	—	0.09	—	0.14	0.07	0.06	—	0.49	—

Continues

Expectations

Satisfaction	Own level income: company	Security	Company status	Intrinsic job	Promotion	'Better opportunities'	Residual
Income	−0.88	—	−0.06	−0.07	−0.07	—	0.81
Security	—	−0.30	—	—	—	—	0.74
Status	−0.20	0.04	−0.24	−0.08	−0.06	−0.07	0.81
Intrinsic job	—	—	—	−0.13	−0.12	—	0.74
Superior	—	—	−0.04	−0.08	−0.03	—	0.62
Social interaction	—	—	—	—	−0.06	−0.05	0.81
Promotion	—	—	−0.05	−0.05	−0.15	−0.17	0.68

NOTE: only those variables have been included where at least one path coefficient has a magnitude of 0.05 or greater.

perceptions of opportunities outside; it is only the situation within the employing establishment or company that matters. Similarly, satisfaction with status is determined more by the individual's perception of his position within the company than by that outside. Finally, satisfaction with intrinsic job rewards depends more upon the extent to which the individual feels that his abilities are used than upon his sense of control.

For the most part, when perceptions and expectations of each reward have been taken into account, there are very few remaining direct effects from background or structural factors. A noticeable exception to this is the respondent's age; older respondents are more satisfied than their younger colleagues, especially with intrinsic job rewards. That this effect not only persists but even increases, despite the fact that both perceptions and expectations have been controlled, strongly indicates that age in itself tends to lead people to express themselves as satisfied. This may perhaps occur because the disjunction between actual and expected rewards is less important, in an absolute sense, for them, or because the element of constrained reality is greater for older respondents in this context than it is when they are directly asked about expectations.

Of the situational, or reward variables, income (in addition to its contribution to satisfaction with income) has a negative influence on satisfaction with intrinsic job. There are a number of other small negative effects from background or structural variables, all of which relate in some way to status, and where at first sight one might expect a positive relationship. Though small, these effects are consistent, and can be explained, we believe, by the fact that satisfactions are less constrained by reality than are expectations.

The major result that emerged from the analysis of cross-effects in the previous chapter was the significance of perceptions of promotion in affecting expectations. As can be seen from Table 5.2 this effect continues strongly when we look at satisfactions. It must be remembered that in the case of perceptions these effects are direct ones – that is after the effects through expectations have been taken into account. The most important influence of perceived promotion prospects is upon satisfaction with income followed by satisfaction with status, intrinsic job, security and social interaction. Expectations with regard to promotion are not, on the whole, as significant, although they do have a depressing effect on satisfaction with everything except security, and this is quite marked for intrinsic job and, together with the 'better opportunities' item, for status. Quite obviously, promotion prospects or expectations do not in themselves make the present job more satisfactory. We have observed the tendency to reduce expectations, but this has been taken account of. Therefore it seems that satisfaction is increased because of the lower salience of present rewards.

Apart from promotion, it is again intrinsic job rewards which stand out. Perceptions of use of abilities and control together have a substantial positive influence on satisfaction with social interaction, superior, promotion and status, while use of abilities alone affects satisfaction with security and income. Intrinsic job expectations have a quite strong negative influence on all of the satisfactions, with the exception of security.

When we looked at the determinants of expectations, the individual's income and his perceptions of the earnings of other groups had very little effect on other rewards. Here, the perceived earnings of the individual's own group in the company, but not his own actual earnings, contribute to satisfaction with status and with intrinsic job rewards. As far as status is concerned there is the usual pattern of perceptions being offset in part by the corresponding expectations, but the influence on intrinsic job rewards is countered by one from the respondent's own income.

The individual's perceptions of his immediate superior play a part, albeit to a fairly limited extent, in his satisfaction with every other aspect of his job, but particularly its intrinsic rewards, where more general social interaction perceptions are also important. His perceived and expected status in the company also tend to influence his satisfaction with income and promotion. Perceptions and expectations of security, however, are relatively unimportant, perhaps reflecting the fact that satisfaction with security was least well related to the other satisfactions. Many of the other cross-effects that we have noted occur where particular satisfactions relate strongly to one another.

Considering expectations, perceptions and satisfactions as a whole, then, it is clear that the greatest spillover from one reward to another is from promotion and from intrinsic job. Promotion is easy to understand since, as we argued earlier, a belief in the likelihood of advancement to a superior position lessens the salience of the individual's present situation, and leads him to lower his expectations and to express himself as more satisfied. The importance of intrinsic job rewards is to a certain extent less expected, and is for that reason perhaps more interesting. As was pointed out earlier, almost all discussions of job satisfaction emphasise the importance of intrinsic job factors, and these results lend further weight to this. It might be argued that the importance of intrinsic rewards has generally emerged because the questions on satisfaction have been answered within the frame of reference of the job as work task, or at least work-place experience, rather than present employment. However, this is quite explicitly not the case here. Not only is the individual's experience of the intrinsic aspects of his work of significance in itself, but it appears also to colour his expectations of and, independently, his satisfaction with other rewards available to him from work.

Satisfaction and salience

Since we have shown the importance of the countervailing effects of rewards, perceptions and expectations upon both satisfactions and, earlier, salience, it is worth extending our analysis to consider these latter two together. In doing this it is not unreasonable to treat satisfaction as an intervening variable. That is, we shall take satisfaction with a particular reward as a direct consequence of the balance between perceptions and expectations, and relative salience as a resolution of competing satisfactions. This necessarily simplifies the process that is occurring, but the results of such an analysis may be sufficiently interesting in themselves. Again, our main interest is in seeing how the different rewards interact with one another.

We would expect, first, a general tendency for salience of a reward to decrease as satisfaction with it increased. In the case of income security, status and intrinsic job this is so, but not for social interaction (Table 5.3). In this last case satisfaction has no significant influence on variations in relative importance, although we should bear in mind both that contact with people was ranked lowest on average, and that satisfaction tends to be consistently high. There is an effect from satisfaction with security, which almost certainly results from a tendency for security to be ranked lower than social interaction when satisfaction with it is higher and vice versa.

In two instances the influence from satisfaction is small, and here the explanation must be, in part at least, the wording that we used in assessing salience. Thus, with status, we referred to the 'respect that comes from doing a socially useful, worthwhile job' which seems not to relate very well to the other measures, which deal with social standing. Similarly, with intrinsic job we referred specifically to use of abilities, and it is this perception, and associated expectations, which

TABLE 5.3 *Satisfaction and salience (path coefficients)*

	Income	Security		Use of abilities	Control	Social interaction perceptions	Superior perceptions	Ought own level income	Desired security income	Intrinsic job expectations	Promotion expectations
		Manual worker	Top manager								
Salience of											
Income	—	—	—	0.09	—	—	—	—	—	—	—
Status	—	0.14	0.09	0.08	—	—	—	—	-0.10	-0.12	—
Security	—	-0.29	-0.14	—	0.05	0.08	-0.05	—	0.25	—	-0.12
Intrinsic job	0.21	—	—	-0.17	-0.07	—	—	-0.15	-0.06	0.24	0.11
Social interaction	—	—	0.06	—	—	-0.11	—	—	—	-0.06	-0.06

continued

	Satisfaction							Residual
	Income	Status	Security	Intrinsic job	Social interaction	Superior	Promotion	
Salience of								
Income	-0.36	-0.13	0.08	0.08	0.06	—	—	0.93
Status	0.09	0.09	0.06	0.01	—	—	—	0.96
Security	0.07	—	-0.23	-0.09	—	0.06	—	0.84
Intrinsic job	0.12	—	0.12	—	—	—	-0.05	0.90
Social interaction	—	—	0.10	—	—	—	—	0.98

is more significant than the more general satisfaction. There is a clear contrast between these two rewards and those of security and income, where the wording on the salience measure was less problematic. In the case of security there are quite strong influences from satisfaction and from perceptions and expectations, while income is the most straightforward of all. Here there is a very strong effect from satisfaction and no additional direct effects from any of the relevant perceptions and expectations.

Because the salience of income and of security are most clearly determined by their respective satisfactions, and because there are certain necessary connections between the different salience measures brought about by the fact that they derive from rankings, these two satisfactions necessarily have a stronger influence on the remaining measures of salience. Even so the effects of satisfaction with one reward on the salience of another are not very marked. In fact it is interesting that in most cases the cross-effects from perceptions and expectations are only slightly reduced by the inclusion of satisfactions. Thus for the most part the results are essentially similar to those noted previously.

Satisfaction and social referents

The results that we have presented suggest that expectations, salience and satisfactions are only to a limited extent determined by the individual's background and social reference groups. Other research findings might lead us to expect otherwise, particularly as regards the importance of the individual's family of origin in determining job satisfaction (e.g. Form and Geschwender, 1962). Such studies have mainly been carried out amongst manual workers, and it may well be that the argument applies much more to this group than it does to non-manual employees. The different social situation of the latter, and their greater experience of career development, lead them to adopt rather broader, less particularistic social referents. Alternatively the answer may be differences in the design and analysis of the research. By introducing a number of intervening variables we have reduced the apparent importance of background factors. In taking account of present circumstances and rewards directly we have shifted the emphasis to current experience and away from earlier social experience.

A further possible explanation of the low importance of family referents is that, given the occupational coverage of our sample, there is greater variability in several of the factors considered than is the case in other studies. So far we have considered the whole range of variables throughout the sample, looking at, for example, the influence of differences in father's occupational status on individuals from a wide variety of backgrounds and in a wide range of present employment. Those whose success is standard, exceptionally high or exceptionally low have thus all been considered together. However, the argument about the importance of reference groups depends not so much on the influence of father's occupational experience throughout the whole range of current positions, as on the hypothesis that for a given position, with a given level of rewards, someone from a lower social status background will tend to express greater satisfaction, perhaps because of lower expectations, than will someone from a higher original status. That is, the argument runs, individuals will select their family of origin (including siblings, whom we have not been able to cover) as a reference in judging their current position and thus their satisfaction.

To study this point adequately, then, one needs to take individuals who are fairly homogeneous with respect to the level of rewards, and compare those from different social backgrounds. In order to look at this question as thoroughly as possible we have chosen those individuals who are at the upper end of our scale of occupational status, taking it that occupational status represents a relatively high level of other rewards. We have looked at two such groups – one made up almost entirely of those in professional occupations, whose score on our status scale is at least 252, and a second rather wider group which includes the first, who have scores of 204 or more. This latter group includes most managers as well as a few more professional groups. The numbers involved are 280 in the first case, and 549 in the second.

For the professional group we find some confirmation of the hypothesis. Amongst this group there is a tendency for those whose fathers are of a higher occupational status to be less satisfied with social interaction, their immediate superior and their status. However, satisfactions with intrinsic job, income and promotion are not significantly affected. On the other hand the social status of the respondent's friends becomes a more positive influence on satisfaction. It ceases to be a negative influence upon satisfaction with status and income, as it tends to be in the total sample, and we find that the higher the status of his friends, the more satisfied he is with social interaction, immediate superior and intrinsic job. These results, however, are probably a consequence of restricting the analysis to respondents in professional occupations. Such occupations, while classified as though homogeneous, actually cover a range of career stages, and thus different status levels within the employing organisation. These are associated with both corresponding levels of rewards and life-styles, which to some extent are reflected in the status of their friends – not all of whom are professionals.

Some support for this argument comes from the fact that though the positive effect remains when we look at the larger group of managers and professionals, it is in a reduced form. The effects from father's occupational status are also reduced in the larger group, except in the case of satisfaction with income, where it now becomes significant. These influences from the status of father and of friends are, of course, acting independently, and directly, upon satisfaction, controlling for expectations. In both cases the effects on expectations themselves are somewhat more pronounced, thus suggesting that the family of origin, at least, does serve as a reference group, albeit a minor one, for our non-manual respondents.

TOTAL SATISFACTION

In moving to a consideration of total satisfaction, that is satisfaction with the job taken as a whole, we are coming closer to the idea of commitment to the employing organisation and thus also to responses which are related to that. Indeed total satisfaction is often taken as the sole indicator of commitment to the organisation, although we prefer to regard it less as an indicator than as a determinant.

Total satisfaction was measured in the same way as all of the specific satisfaction items, that is by asking the individual to indicate his position on a line with verbal descriptions at a number of points. He was asked to indicate his position, taking into account all aspects of his job. The mean response was a score of 35, approximately mid-way in the range of means for satisfaction with the individual items.

Earlier in the chapter we considered levels of satisfaction with various aspects of the job and the relations between them. Now that we have come to look at total satisfaction, the question naturally arises of how far each of the individual satisfactions contributes to total satisfaction, and how these relative contributions relate to the importance of the items. There have been a substantial number of studies of job satisfaction concerned with problems of this kind, many of them directed at a test of Herzberg's hypothesis of distinguishable

TABLE 5.4 *Influences on total satisfaction (path coefficients)*

(a) Individual satisfactions only

Income	Status	Security	Intrinsic job	Social interaction	Superior	Promotion	Residual
0.10	0.08	0.06	0.38	0.11	0.07	0.28	0.61

(b) Background and present location

Age	Service in firm	Number of dependents	Friends' status	Use of abilities	Control	Promotion perceptions	'Opportunities outside'	Security: Manual worker	Security: Top manager	Superior perceptions	Social interaction perceptions	Residual
0.12	−0.06	−0.04	−0.06	0.25	0.14	0.28	−0.08	0.05	0.07	0.11	0.11	0.77

(c) All factors

Others' time	Company status	Security: top manager	Use of abilities	Control	Superior perceptions	Satisfaction Income	Status	Security	Intrinsic job	Social interaction	Superior	Promotion	Residual
0.04	−0.03	0.04	0.08	0.04	−0.06	0.10	0.09	0.04	0.35	0.11	0.11	0.27	0.60

satisfiers and dissatisfiers. We shall begin by considering, very simply, the contributions overall of the individual satisfactions, and then go on to see whether our respondents can be broken down in some way, such that different groups can be separately considered.

The path coefficients of the individual satisfactions on total satisfaction are shown in Table 5.4(a). This shows quite clearly that, as with most other studies of this kind, by far the most important single contribution comes from satisfaction with intrinsic job. This is followed by satisfaction with promotion. Satisfaction with social interaction, income, status, supervision and security are markedly less important.

These results, however, are based on the assumption that total satisfaction is dependent solely upon the individual satisfactions, and unspecified variables which are unrelated to them (the residual path). In particular it assumes that all the background and other variables we have previously considered operate only through these satisfactions. Before putting this assumption to the test it is worth looking at the relationship between total satisfaction and background factors, present location and perceptions, as shown in Table 5.4(b). This makes clear what we would expect from the results given in Table 5.4(a), that the intrinsic job rewards, or at least the perceptions of the degree to which the job allows use of abilities and control, are very important. So also are perceptions of promotion prospects. Where opportunities within the company are seen to be good, satisfaction is considerably greater, but it is predictably less when those outside are favourably perceived. The other important perceptions are those of the immediate superior and of social interaction, and it is interesting that none of the variables relating to either income or status seem to be significant, with the exception of the status of the respondent's friends. Those with higher earnings were more satisfied with both income and status, and we would therefore expect some relationship here. Perhaps in this case it has been largely mediated through the intrinsic job and promotion perceptions, since the former particularly are substantially determined by structural location.

When the individual satisfactions are again introduced into the analysis we find that our first assumption that they are alone sufficient is, in fact, to a large extent justified. Only a few other variables have any continuing significant direct effects on total satisfaction, and these are fairly small, although the existence of one at least is nevertheless interesting. What we find is that even controlling for satisfactions, those who have more favourable perceptions of the use of abilities that their jobs allow still tend to be more satisfied overall. We saw earlier that expectations and perceptions of intrinsic job rewards had an extensive influence on satisfaction with other specific aspects of the job. It appears that the contribution to satisfaction of rewards of this kind is much more general and diffuse than their effects on satisfaction with that particular aspect alone. Including these variables has little effect on the size of the paths from the individual satisfactions already given, or on that from other variables (the residual path).

In view of our earlier finding that intrinsic job and income were rated about equal in importance by our respondents, it is interesting to note the considerable discrepancy between intrinsic job satisfaction and satisfaction with income in determining total satisfaction. Equally interesting is the significance of satisfaction with social interaction, remembering that only for a very few respondents was this aspect of the job the most salient. On the other hand, security, which was on average more salient, has a very much smaller influence on total satisfaction. Given the fact that on the whole our respondents are comparatively well satisfied, this result might be explained by Herzberg's (1968) hypothesis that certain factors operate as positive satisfiers, whilst others can be regarded simply as 'hygiene' factors, where a high value has no effect but a low value leads to dissatisfaction. Certainly our findings with respect to intrinsic job on the one hand and income on the other, lend credence to this view. This is increased by the strong effect from satisfaction with promotion, but decreased by the apparently weak influence of satisfaction with status.

The simplest interpretation of Herzberg is to distinguish those aspects of the job that respondents like, which therefore must be satisfiers, from those that they dislike, the dissatisfiers. This implies both that there is a consensus among respondents as to which aspects come into each category, and that the ranges of satisfaction within each would differ, such that high levels of satisfaction would be excluded for the dissatisfiers and vice versa. In fact the data do not support any such arguments, and certainly not that of Herzberg, as can be seen from the relative order of means of satisfaction, with security, a hygiene factor, having the highest level.

However this is a narrow interpretation of Herzberg and not the only one possible. A more adequate test of his hypotheses, using our data, may be made by considering two groups of respondents – those who are substantially more satisfied than average and those correspondingly less satisfied: roughly these are the upper and lower

quartiles. If Herzberg were correct, the influences on overall satisfaction would come from the 'dissatisfied' scores on 'hygiene' factors
and the 'satisfied' scores on satisfiers – the remainder of each scale
having no effect; thus we should find that amongst the highly satisfied
group the most important determinants of satisfaction are the so-
called satisfiers, whereas amongst the dissatisfied group the hygiene
factors would be of more significance. The two groups cannot be
taken to be differentiated by the separate operation of these two types
of factors since satisfaction or dissatisfaction cannot be taken as
resulting from the effects solely of satisfying or dissatisfying aspects
of the job. However it seems clear that there must be a strong relationship.

The results are shown in Table 5.5(a). Of those factors which can
clearly be identified as 'satisfiers' in Herzberg's scheme – intrinsic job,
status and promotion – one, status, has more or less equal influence in
both groups. In the case of the other two the relative influence is
actually greater amongst the dissatisfied group than amongst the
satisfied. Conversely, when we look at the clearly identifiable
'hygiene' factors – security and income – we find that the relative
effect of security is much greater amongst the highly satisfied.
Although the effect of income is, in both cases, scarcely significant, it
is a little higher, again, amongst the highly satisfied.

Since path coefficients reflect the amount of variation in a
particular variable in a population, it might be argued that these
results are not conclusive. That is, they could be accounted for by the
fact that among the less satisfied there is a greater variability in some
satisfactions compared with others than there is among the more
satisfied. However, since we are dealing with variables all of which
have been measured in a comparable way with similar units, we can in
this case compare the unstandardised regression coefficients, which
are also shown in the table. The results in fact are very similar to those
found with the path coefficients. In the highly satisfied group, the
largest coefficients are those of intrinsic job, social interaction and
promotion, while amongst the low satisfied group the largest are from
intrinsic job, promotion and status. As can be seen, the coefficients
are on the whole rather larger in the latter case.

Thus these results give no support to Herzberg, nor to the general
idea that one can distinguish certain satisfiers, which are likely to have
a greater effect amongst the highly satisfied, from hygiene factors,
which would have a greater effect amongst those whose satisfaction is
low. Rather, it appears to be the case that the same variables, and

TABLE 5.5 Influences on total satisfaction: (a) satisfied and dissatisfied separately, and (b) non-linear effects (path coefficients, with the unstandardised regression coefficients in parentheses)

	Income	Status	Security	Intrinsic job	Social interaction	Superior	Promotion	Residual (R^2)
(a) Dissatisfied	0.01*	0.10	0.01*	0.33	0.05*	0.10	0.31	0.79
($N = 473$)	(0.01)	(0.07)	(0.01)	(0.21)	(0.04)	(0.06)	(0.20)	(0.38)
Satisfied	0.05*	0.10	0.12	0.24	0.11	0.08*	0.16	0.85
($N = 494$)	(0.02)	(0.05)	(0.05)	(0.15)	(0.07)	(0.04)	(0.07)	(0.28)
(b) Linear	0.19	−0.01*	0.19	0.64	0.19	0.18	0.39	0.60
	(0.15)	(−0.01)	(0.18)	(0.62)	(0.21)	(0.16)	(0.33)	
Quadratic	−0.08*	0.10*	−0.12*	−0.26	−0.07*	−0.12*	−0.12	(0.64)
	(−0.0012)	(0.0014)	(−0.0015)	(−0.0038)	(−0.0010)	(−0.0015)	(−0.0018)	

* Not significant at the 1 per cent level.

notably intrinsic job satisfaction, are important for both the satisfied and the dissatisfied.

There is another way of approaching this question which uses the whole sample. If Herzberg is correct, or more generally if there are any factors which operate as hygiene factors or satisfiers, then we would expect to find that where satisfaction is low the hygiene factors would be having the most important influence, but that their effect would decrease as total satisfaction increases. This would imply that, overall, the effect would be a relationship expressed by a curve which began steeply and flattened out. (In an extreme, and most simple form, a steep line which turned at some point to a horizontal one.) In contrast, for the satisfiers we would expect a curve which began fairly flat amongst the low satisfied, and became steeper as satisfaction increased. If we tried to fit a quadratic curve, rather than the usual straight line, to the regression of the total on the individual satisfactions, we should get a coefficient for the squared term which was negative for the hygiene factors and positive for the satisfiers.

In fact what we find when we do this (Table 5.5(b) and as illustrated in Figure 5.1) is that only two of the coefficients of the squared term are significant at the 1 per cent level; those for intrinsic job and

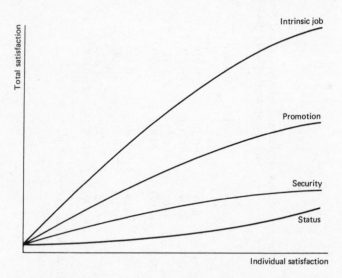

Note: Each line has been drawn using the multiple regression coefficients, and assuming that
the intercept terms are equal. For clarity the vertical scale has been magnified by a
factor of approximately 70 per cent.

FIGURE 5.1   *Non-linear regression of individual on total satisfaction*

promotion satisfaction. Both of those, contrary to what we would expect to happen for satisfiers, are negative. The only positive coefficient is for satisfaction with status, where the linear term itself disappears. Though its overall influence on total satisfaction is slight this does appear to be a candidate for a satisfier. Income and security can, on this evidence, be classed as hygiene factors, but less clearly than intrinsic job rewards and promotion! Overall, the introduction of the squared terms adds very little to the explanation.

Any attempt to divide job characteristics into satisfiers and dissatisfiers seems highly dubious, and in particular that of Herzberg is unquestionably wrong. Thus, we have seen that at least one attempt to specify in advance the important determinants of satisfaction is not successful.

What, though, of the individual's own assessment of the importance of a particular reward, and the relative influence of that reward upon total satisfaction? We might expect to find that the more important a reward is for an individual, the greater is the effect of satisfaction with that reward upon satisfaction with the job as a whole. However, this has not been the case in a considerable amount of previous work, where importance has been measured in a somewhat different way, i.e. more abstractly in terms of the importance attributed directly to the various aspects (see Smith, Kendal and Hulin, 1969; Quinn and Mangione, 1973). One exception to this is the work of Beynon and Blackburn (1972), but there satisfaction with rewards is measured rather differently, or rather replaced by workers' assessments of how well certain needs were catered for by the job. When account is taken of importance this is somewhat closer to our emphasis on improvements.

Our results, presented in Table 5.6, show that relative importance, as measured in terms of marginal improvements, does have some influence on the contribution of satisfaction with an individual reward to total satisfaction. In one case, that of security, we find that comparing those who regard it as important and those who regard it as unimportant there is a considerable difference in the size of the path coefficients, in the direction anticipated. However, in no other instance is the effect anything like as marked as this. In the case of income, the coefficient is about 2½ times as great, with social interaction twice as great, and with intrinsic job, just a little more. With status, there is in fact a reversal, so that the influence of satisfaction with status is actually greater when this factor is considered to be of low importance.

TABLE 5.6 Contribution of individual satisfactions to total satisfaction according to salience (path coefficients)

Salience	N	Satisfaction							Residual
		Income	Status	Security	Intrinsic job	Social interaction	Superior	Promotion	
Income									
Important	708	0.17	0.12	0.06	0.35	0.08	0.09	0.22	0.62
Not important	286	0.07	0.02	0.02	0.40	0.22	−0.01	0.30	0.61
Status									
Important	495	0.12	0.01	0.05	0.46	0.12	0.06	0.25	0.61
Not important	421	0.11	0.12	0.11	0.39	0.10	0.01	0.26	0.64
Security									
Important	489	0.04	0.10	0.18	0.27	0.07	0.09	0.30	0.68
Not important	691	0.09	0.10	−0.01	0.40	0.13	0.08	0.30	0.56
Intrinsic job									
Important	736	0.07	0.10	0.02	0.39	0.12	0.08	0.32	0.55
Not important	325	0.13	0.02	0.12	0.35	0.07	0.09	0.25	0.71
Social interaction									
Important	340	0.09	0.09	−0.02	0.41	0.20	−0.00	0.30	0.56
Not important	581	0.14	0.03	0.10	0.35	0.09	0.11	0.26	0.62

NOTE: 'Important' means ranked first for intrinsic job and income, and ranked first or second for the remainder. 'Not important' means ranked fourth or fifth for intrinsic job and income, and ranked fifth for the remainder. The different bases of categorisation were used in order to avoid small numbers and to ensure more comparable groupings.

The results of this section on satisfaction indicate very clearly the importance of two major factors. One is the nature of the work task, as this is given by the two intrinsic job rewards: use of abilities and control. This aspect of work contributes more than any other to total satisfaction, and even spills over into satisfaction with other aspects of the job. This last is true also of promotion. As we saw in the previous chapter, those who see better prospects of advancement with their present employer have lower expectations of current rewards; now we find that they are also more satisfied. Thus a belief in promotion acts as a means of coming to terms with the present situation because it holds out the prospect of personal change within the existing structure of the organisation leading to increases in future rewards. In the next section we shall consider the other responses that are available to the individual.

INDIVIDUAL ADAPTATIONS TO UNSATISFACTORY CONDITIONS

We have argued that promotion can be taken as an indicator of positive commitment to the employing organisation, or at least to the form of employment. An expectation of promotion involves a willingness to leave the current situation, but a positive acceptance of the structure of employment. We want to look in this section at two forms of adaptation to unsatisfactory features of employment which reflect low commitment to work and/or the employing organisation. These are job attachment – or rather its inverse, the propensity to leave – and self-estrangement. However, before discussing these we can look at a more direct indicator of commitment to the organisation. This is the individual's attitude towards the top management in his company. It must be recognised that this is a less than perfect indicator since one has to distinguish between on the one hand the individual's attachment to an organisation and what he sees as its objectives, and on the other hand his attitude toward those who happen to be in top management positions within it.

Attitude to top management

A measure of attitudes to top management was constructed out of two separate items. They are: (1) 'This company is very fair to its employees', and (2) 'Top management in this company has no under-

TABLE 5.7 Influences on attitude to top management (path coefficients)

(a) Background and situational factors

Age	First job status	Present job status	Attendance at political associations	Superiors: number	Others: time	Own level income: Company	Own level income: Society	Company status	Security: Own level worker	Security: Manual worker	Promotion perceptions	Superior perceptions	Social interaction perceptions	Residual
0.15	−0.05	−0.07	−0.04	0.05	0.04	0.34	−0.25	0.12	0.07	0.05	0.30	0.13	0.08	0.84

(b) Including expectations and individual satisfactions

Age	First job status	Attendance at political associations	Superiors: number	Others: time	Company status	Use of abilities	Control	Superior perceptions	Promotion status	Desired status	Intrinsic job expectations	Satisfaction: Income	Satisfaction: Security	Satisfaction: Superior	Satisfaction: Social interaction	Residual
0.15	−0.07	0.05	0.05	0.12	0.07	0.05	0.15	0.22	−0.06		−0.06	0.19	0.15	−0.10	0.09	0.81

(c) Including total satisfaction

Age	First job status	Attendance at political associations	Company status	Superior perceptions	Promotion perceptions	Security expectations	Intrinsic job expectations	Promotion expectations	Satisfaction: Income	Satisfaction: Security	Satisfaction: Superior	Satisfaction: Social interaction	Satisfaction: Total	Residual
0.14	−0.07	0.04	0.09	0.18	0.20	−0.04	−0.06	0.06	0.17	0.14	−0.13	0.07	0.17	0.80

(d) Public employment

Type of school	Own level income	Superior perceptions	Promotion perceptions	Ought own level income	Intrinsic job expectations	Satisfaction				Residual
						Income	Security	Superior	Total	
-0.10	0.43	0.40	0.18	-0.34	-0.17	0.05	0.14	-0.22	0.30	0.75

(e) Private employment

Age	First job status	Attendance at political associations	Others: status	Company time	Promotion perceptions	Superior perceptions	Promotion expectations	Security expectations	Satisfaction			Residual
									Income	Security	Total	
0.17	-0.07	0.06	0.05	0.11	0.08	0.21	-0.05	0.06	0.17	0.15	0.14	0.80

standing of our problems'. The extent of agreement with each was measured on a scale from 1 to 5, with 3 representing a neutral response. The mean score on the first item was 3.7, indicating that most people tend to agree; and on the second, 2.8, showing a lesser tendency for them to disagree. In constructing a composite measure the individual's scores on the two items were simply added together, of course taking account of the fact that the second statement is negative.

Considering, to begin with, just background or situational factors (Table 5.7(a)), the major influences on attitudes to top management are opposing positive and negative ones from perceptions of the income of their own group in the company and outside, and a positive one from perception of promotion prospects. Also important are age and perceptions of company status and immediate supervisors. All these are in line with what we might expect from previous discussion, though it is interesting to note that in this case there is no significant effect from perceptions of intrinsic job rewards.

When expectations and individual satisfactions are introduced into the analysis (Table 5.7(b)) the main influences remain, apart from perceptions of income which is replaced by the effect of satisfaction. In addition there are contributions from satisfaction with security and to a lesser extent social interaction. The rather curious negative influence from satisfaction with immediate superiors has to be considered in conjunction with the opposing one from the corresponding perceptions.

When total satisfaction is included (Table 5.7(c)) it has, as we would expect, a fairly substantial influence. Otherwise the pattern remains much the same, with several noteworthy continuing influences. Age is interesting when one considers that it also had an independent effect on the individual satisfactions, some of which have been taken into account directly, and all of which are included indirectly through their influence on total satisfaction. The magnitude of this direct effect, and the fact that, as can be seen by comparing parts (a), (b), and (c) of Table 5.7, its relative influence is scarcely affected by the introduction of other factors, provides yet more evidence of the great importance of age.

The largest single influence on attitude to top management comes from perceptions of promotion. This is evidence, even more convincing than that given previously, of the way in which perceived opportunity to participate in the upper levels of the organisation, and thus confidence in promotion, contributes to a high identification with those in top positions and, we would argue, to a high degree of attachment to the organisation. It is interesting that it is perceptions themselves which are important, and not satisfaction with promotion. However the direct effect is slightly reduced by the inclusion of total satisfaction.

The other very important point which emerges is that levels of satisfaction with some of the individual rewards still exercise an influence, even when their indirect effects through total satisfaction have been taken into account. Others, notably satisfaction with intrinsic job rewards, are not significant even when the latter is omitted. In particular, satisfaction with income actually has as strong an influence on attitude to top management as does total satisfaction, and we also find that satisfaction with security is of significance. It is important to stress this in view of the way in which satisfaction with the job as a whole has often been used as an indicator of commitment. The effect that satisfaction with income has had on this alternative indicator strongly suggests that studies which apparently demonstrate the lack of importance of income and security are mistaken. It also sheds an interesting light on the question of the effect of salience, since it will be recalled that income was generally ranked as one of the most important rewards, while its contribution to total satisfaction was limited. This is part of a general pattern. When we come to consider variables which also reflect commitment to the organisation, we shall find as we do here that different rewards are more or less significant in each particular case. While total satisfaction is undoubtedly of interest in itself, it is far from being the only useful indicator, and probably not the best, of commitment, and thus on its own a misleading basis for generalisation.

It is interesting to compare those in private and public employment. Although there is no significant difference between the mean values in the two sectors an analysis of covariance shows that when other factors are allowed for there is a significantly more favourable general attitude to top management amongst public employees.

The necessity for a separate treatment is clear from the differences between parts (d) and (e) of Table 5.7. The results for private employment are close to the overall pattern because this group constitutes a large majority of the sample, so our comments will be restricted to those in the public sector. Perhaps the most notable point as far as they are concerned is the replacement of satisfaction with income by, on the one hand, total satisfaction and, on the other, joint opposing effects from actual and expected income. Perceptions of, and satisfaction with, the individual's superior are also more significant than for those employed in the private sector. Taken together these results suggest that top management is likely to be blamed not only for its own shortcomings, but also for its influence on income distribution.

Job attachment

Five items were used in the construction, using factor analysis, of the job attachment measure. They are (with their loadings in parentheses):

(1) 'Sometimes it is not really worthwhile working hard at my job' (0.62).
(2) 'I get highly involved in my work and put in a great deal of effort' (−0.37).
(3) 'I sometimes feel that I would prefer not to come to work' (0.48).
(4) 'I would leave this job at once if I had another to go to' (0.69).
(5) 'I have been seriously considering moving to another job' (0.65).

As can be seen there are really three aspects to this composite measure. The first two items relate to the effort that the individual puts into his job, the third to feelings of temporary avoidance, and the last two to more permanent avoidance by moving elsewhere. The factor loading of the five items indicates that it is the third of these aspects which is central.

There is a high average level of agreement with the only positive item, the second one, while the mean level of agreement with the first, third and fifth items is between the 'disagree' and 'neither agree nor disagree' categories. There is rather more disagreement on average with the fourth item.

The determinants of job attachment are shown in Table 5.8. As before the table is presented in five parts. The first three are essentially consistent, except that when total satisfaction is included (c) we also introduce significant opposing influences from perceptions and expectations of income. We can see that total satisfaction does have the most significant effect, and this almost certainly reflects the fact that job attachment results from the individual's involvement in the work that he is doing in itself, as well as from his commitment to the organisation. This is evidenced by the influence of intrinsic job satisfaction and, in addition to this, direct effects from perceptions of use of abilities and control. Social interaction perceptions, too, which are also an aspect of the job itself, have some influence. Bearing in mind that intrinsic job rewards are important determinants of total satisfaction, these results are of considerable interest. The importance of this aspect of the job is most clearly demonstrated if we ignore total satisfaction as a possible factor in job attachment, regarding it simply as another indicator of commitment. We find then that intrinsic job satisfaction is the most important determinant as also, when only background factors and rewards are considered, are the perceptions of the use made of the individual's abilities and of his degree of control.

The other aspect of job attachment, which is indicated more by those items concerned with the propensity to move elsewhere, is more likely to account for the fact that this variable is positively affected by perceptions of promotion, and negatively by the 'good opportunities outside' item. That is, those who see good chances elsewhere are less likely to wish to remain in their present job, and those who see good promotion prospects within the company are more likely to do so. Again, when total satisfaction is ignored the influence of satisfaction with promotion appears more strongly. When that itself is omitted the full effect of perceptions of promotions shows up very clearly. The importance of outside opportunities in reducing attachment to the present job raises certain problems regarding this item and its relationship to commitment. In particular it points up the problem of trying to understand promotion as a personal strategy. On the one hand, while a lack of opportunities within the organisation may well help reduce the degree of commitment, on the other, variations in outside circumstances may be unrelated to the internal factors which affect this.

The main factors not related to the individual's present position are age and level of qualifications. The effect of age is, again, quite a marked one, once more demonstrating the importance of this factor. Level of qualifications, perhaps surprisingly, has a negative effect; that is, the better-qualified have lower job attachment. This may reflect the fact that their jobs are not making full use of what they perceive to be their abilities, or simply that those with formal qualifications are more able to move to comparable or better jobs, possibly identifying more with a (professional) occupation than an employer.

In fact, however, this effect is not significant for either public or private employees when each is dealt with separately. As before, for those in the public sector there is a stronger effect from total satisfaction. What otherwise distinguishes this group is that among them years of service replace age, and that job attachment is greater among

TABLE 5.8 *Influences on job attachment (path coefficients)*

(a) Background and situational factors

Age	Qualific- ations	Friends' status	Subordinates		Company status	Security		Use of abilities	Control	Superior perceptions	Social interaction perceptions
			Number	Time		Own level	Manual worker				
0.19	−0.07	−0.05	0.05	−0.04	0.05	0.04	0.05	0.29	0.10	0.08	0.10

(b) Including expectations and individual satisfactions

Age	Qualifi- cations	Married	Use of abilities	Control	Social interaction perceptions	Promotion perceptions	'Opportunities outside'	Security expectations	Promotion expectations
0.14	−0.08	0.04	0.20	0.05	0.04	0.13	−0.09	0.04	0.04

(c) Including total satisfaction

Age	Qualific- ations	Married	Distance moved	Subordinates		Own level income	Company status	Use of abilities	Control	Superior perceptions
				Time	Number					
0.14	−0.07	0.04	0.03	0.03	0.05	0.11	0.04	0.19	0.04	0.04

(d) Public employment

First job status	Service in firm	Superiors: time	Use of abilities	Social interaction perceptions	Satisfaction		Residual
					Social interaction	Total	
−0.12	0.14	−0.08	0.23	0.18	−0.12	0.57	0.63

(e) Private employment

Age	Part-time (evening) further education	Subordinates: number	Own level income	Security: own level	Use of abilities	Control	'Opportunities outside'	Superior perceptions	Social interaction perceptions
0.22	−0.55	0.06	0.12	0.04	0.18	0.04	−0.08	0.04	0.05

Promotion perceptions	'Opportunities outside'	Residual
0.25	−0.12	0.74

		Satisfaction			Residual
Income	Security	Intrinsic job	Superior	Promotion	
0.09	0.05	0.18	0.05	0.15	0.70

Social interaction perceptions	Promotion perceptions	'Opportunities outside'	Ought own level income	Security expectations	Satisfaction				Residual
					Income	Security	Intrinsic job	Total	
0.06	0.13	−0.08	−0.15	0.03	0.03	0.03	0.05	0.35	0.67

Promotion perceptions	Ought own level income	Security expectations	Promotion expectations	'Better opportunities'	Satisfaction			Residual
					Income	Security	Total	
0.13	0.16	0.04	0.05	−0.06	0.04	0.05	0.34	0.67

those who started in lower-status positions. Again, although the overall difference between the two fields of employment is not significant, allowing for other influences suggests greater job attachment on the part of the publicly employed.

Self-estrangement

Given the difficult and complex nature of the concept of self-estrangement we decided to make use of an existing measure rather than attempt to develop our own. Naturally, this was satisfactory only in so far as we considered what was available as adequate for our theoretical purposes. Before considering the correctness of this judgement we should look at the items which go to make up the scale, which are shown below with their factor loadings:

(1) 'I have found that, in order to get along at work, you have to put on an act instead of being able to be your real self' (0.70).
(2) 'What others think I should do is usually not what I would really like to do' (0.60).
(3) 'I frequently have to do things to please others that I would rather not do' (0.61).
(4) 'When I am with other people I try to keep in mind that saying what you really feel often gets you into trouble' (0.52).
(5) 'I have found that just being your natural self won't get you very far in your job' (0.69).
(6) 'Sometimes I get restless because I can't express my real feelings when talking and doing things with others' (0.54).

These six items have been taken over almost unchanged from Bonjean and Grimes (1970) who treated them as one element in a measure of alienation. However, this term has by now taken on so many meanings that it is very dangerous to use it in any specific instance, since it is likely to convey to many readers intentions that the authors may not have had. In the present case, alienation is also a poor term to use because it is not directly related to the main tradition of the concept. To some extent it has been altered, more or less subtly, in attempting to operationalise it in sociological research, and there has been a tendency for it to have become too psychological and to have lost much of its sociological content (Horton, 1964). It thus fails to take adequate account of the objective features of the situation in which the psychological characteristics arise, in particular the external forces which constrain individuals. Foremost among the latter are social constraints which are reinforced by the individual's own cognitions of the social world.

Although these items do not provide a measure of alienation, they can arguably be taken to measure one possible consequence or aspect of it. They clearly refer to a form of self-estrangement, that is the more or less conscious use of the self as an object without a direct and authentic involvement in the situation. The process is more, rather than less, conscious in so far as agreement with these statements does depend on a degree of self-awareness. Again it is arguable to what extent alienation requires this degree of consciousness, but the concept loses much of its dynamic possibility if none at all were thought to be normal. The idea of self-estrangement, especially, seems to require it, though it is true that the measure used here may confuse a cynical form of self-estrangement, consciously used by the individual, perhaps as a means of ingratiating or advancing himself, with that form which more clearly constitutes avoidance of the situation. It is the latter in which we are primarily interested, and the set of items, taken as a whole, appear to relate essentially to this form of psychological withdrawal.

On average, our respondents disagree with all six of these items. They disagree most strongly with the first of them; less strongly with the third, fifth and sixth; and are very close to the middle, 'neither agree nor disagree' category with the second and fourth. The determinants of self-estrangement are shown in Table 5.9, in five sections as before, and again the main influence is total satisfaction. Those who are more satisfied with their job tend to be much less self-estranged. The other major determinant, again negative, is the perceived status in the company, together with an additional effect from our own measure of the status of the respondent's job. Thus it is those lower in status, and especially at lower levels in the organisation, who are most likely to experience this sense of estrangement. However it also tends to be those who desire a higher level of status. Perceived company status has the same kind of effect when background factors alone are considered, but it is increased with the introduction of expectations and satisfactions. It appears to be the discrepancy between perceptions and expectations which is important, mainly directly and, to a much smaller extent, through satisfaction with status.

There is a similar pattern for intrinsic job rewards. Here again, those whose jobs enable less use of their abilities and provide less

TABLE 5.9 *Influences on self-estrangement (path coefficients)*

(a) Background and situational factors

Married	Number of moves	Service in firm	Subordinates: time	Others: time	Company status	Use of abilities	Control
−0.06	0.05	0.10	0.06	0.05	−0.14	−0.18	−0.10

(b) Including expectations and individual satisfactions

Married	Number of moves	Service in firm	Present job status	Company status	Subordinates: time	Use of abilities	Control	Superior perceptions
−0.09	0.06	0.08	−0.06	−0.16	0.04	−0.21	−0.11	−0.07

(c) Including total satisfaction

Father non-manual	Married	Number of moves	Service in firm	Present job status	Subordinates: time	Others: time	Company status	Use of abilities	Control	Superior perceptions
−0.04	−0.09	0.06	0.08	−0.06	0.05	0.04	−0.17	−0.17	−0.09	−0.06

(d) Public employment

Use of abilities	Superior perceptions	Satisfaction		Residual
		Income	Total	
−0.18	−0.16	0.12	−0.49	0.78

(e) Private employment

Father non-manual	Married	Number of moves	Service in firm	Present job status	Company status	Use of abilities	Control	Superior perceptions
−0.06	−0.09	0.07	0.08	−0.06	−0.18	−0.16	−0.08	−0.06

Security: top manager	Promotion perceptions	'Opportunities outside'	Superior perceptions	Social interaction perceptions	Residual
−0.05	−0.12	0.08	−0.11	−0.10	0.86

Social interaction perceptions	Desired status	Intrinsic job expectations	Promotion expectations	'Better opportunities'	Satisfaction				Residual
					Status	*Security*	*Intrinsic job*	*Social interaction*	
−0.06	0.11	0.15	−0.10	0.09	−0.07	−0.07	−0.08	−0.07	0.83

Social interaction perceptions	Desired status	Intrinsic job expectations	Promotion expectations	'Better opportunities'	Satisfaction		Residual
					Security	Total	
−0.07	0.12	0.14	−0.11	0.06	−0.05	0.28	0.81

Social interaction perceptions	Desired status	Intrinsic job expectations	Promotion expectations	'Better opportunities'	Total satisfaction	Residual
−0.07	0.13	0.13	−0.11	0.08	−0.27	0.82

control, and who have higher expectations, are more psychologically withdrawn. Even though total satisfaction is very much influenced by intrinsic job rewards, its introduction only slightly weakens the direct effect from perceptions and expectations. It is clear that the perceptions and expectations of intrinsic job and status rewards have an effect on self-estrangement which is separate from, and largely independent of, their effect on satisfaction. Thus the influence of the individual satisfactions is small, although there is quite a strong relationship with the overall sense of satisfaction.

While none of the other influences is very strong, both promotion prospects and social interaction do have some effect. When only background factors and perceptions are considered we see that perceptions of good promotion prospects reduce the degree of self-estrangement but these give way to expectations when the latter are introduced, reflecting the nature of promotion as an alternative experience. Perceptions of superiors and social interaction, and satisfaction with the latter all reduce psychological withdrawal as we would expect, but time spent with subordinates and colleagues tends to have the opposite effect. Although the coefficients are quite small there is also an indication that those who are married tend to feel less estrangement, while those who have moved often and are of longer service feel more.

The importance of status, intrinsic job rewards and promotion suggests that one group likely to experience greater self-estrangement are those who have failed to gain significant promotion, and examination of those in the top quartile supports this. These are people for whom the apparent predictability of the social world has broken down, and who are left doing inferior jobs without, perhaps, any clear understanding of why they have failed. Thus they attribute to the world of work the characteristic of denying 'real' human nature, and to their more successful colleagues that of putting on an act. In this way they are able to lessen the significance of work and their own real involvement in it. The other group that the conjunction of characteristics suggests is that of manual workers who have moved into the less rewarding non-manual jobs, and might be expected to share a more general working-class alienated view of employment. Interestingly, however, this group is not significantly more self-estranged.

Explanation is both more adequate and more parsimonious for those employed in the public sector. This is one case where there is a significant difference in the means between the two fields of employment, with those in the private sector exhibiting greater self-estrangement. Amongst the publicly employed there is a very strong effect from total satisfaction, and relatively strong ones from use of abilities and perceptions of the immediate superior. All three are negative, as in private employment.

We have previously argued that there are complex relationships of perceptions and expectations to satisfaction with various rewards. In this chapter we have seen that this applies equally to other outcomes, and to their relations with satisfaction. The basic point is that different outcomes are influenced by different rewards, either by perceptions and expectations directly or through satisfaction. Self-estrangement, as we have just seen, is largely influenced directly by intrinsic job and status. The main rewards affecting job attachment are intrinsic job and promotion, operating both directly and through satisfaction. Perceptions of promotion and of the immediate superior are influences on attitudes to top management, but otherwise the most important effects are from satisfaction, particularly income and security. Finally, total satisfaction is almost entirely determined by individual satisfactions, in this case intrinsic job and promotion. When total satisfaction is included as a possible determinant of the other outcomes, it is usually amongst the most important. In the case of job attachment it mostly replaces the individual satisfactions, but this is not so with attitude to top management. How far it is valid to include total satisfaction in this way is an issue that we shall take up in the next chapter when we consider the more general question of the relationships between outcomes.

Another point which develops arguments made in the previous chapter is the continuing significance of age. As we showed, older respondents tend to have lower expectations, but even allowing for this they tend also to express greater satisfaction. Linking this with an earlier argument it seems likely that with age there comes a closer relation between expectations and wants, that is an increasing extension of realistic constraints into less consciously formulated areas. What is more, even allowing for this increased satisfaction, older respondents not only exhibit stronger job attachment, which is not surprising in view of their restricted opportunities to move elsewhere, but more favourable attitudes towards the top management in their company.

The importance of perceptions of promotion opportunities and of intrinsic job rewards, particularly the extent to which the respondent felt that his job made use of his abilities, also began to emerge in the previous chapter, and the significance of these two rewards has been further confirmed in the present one. Not only do the perceptions and expectations have an effect on satisfaction with other aspects of the job, but satisfaction with promotion and with intrinsic job rewards are the major determinants of total satisfaction. These two rewards are also among the major factors in determining job attachment and self-estrangement, both of which are essentially individualistic. In the following chapter we shall consider how far they affect collective adaptations, and how the collective and the individual forms relate to one another.

6 Attitudes Towards Collective Representation

In this chapter we turn to a consideration of collective representation. Up to now our analysis has been confined to individual adaptations or experiences. Here we shall be concerned with efforts to change the situation rather than to avoid it. Firstly we deal with two variables related to the individual's propensity to participate in an association whose objectives include such a change. We consider separately that which we refer to as enterprise unionateness, concerned with change simply within the employing organisation, and society unionateness, which relates to society more widely. Both may also be regarded as indicators of commitment to a union or other representative organisation for those who are members, but the attitudes relate to general preferences and do not require any organisation to be available, let alone joined. Thus what we are concerned with here is not actual collective strategies, but individual attitudes reflecting propensity. In this sense they are comparable to the individual adaptations dealt with in the previous chapter, and we shall be concerned with showing the relationships between them. The question of involvement in collective organisations will be taken up in the companion volume to this one.

UNIONATENESS

The development of the concept of unionateness in our work, and the ways in which we have attempted to measure the two aspects of it that we distinguish, has been fully described in a previous publication, and those interested in the details of the techniques by which the measures of society and enterprise unionateness were constructed may consult that article (Prandy, Stewart and Blackburn, 1974).

The concept was introduced by one of the authors (Blackburn, 1967; Blackburn and Prandy, 1965) as a means of dealing with the character of organisations. An organisation was to be described as more or less unionate 'according to the extent to which it is a whole-hearted trade union, identifying with the labour movement and willing to use all the powers of the movement' (Blackburn, 1967, 18) and the level of unionateness 'depends on the commitment of an organisation to the general principles and ideology of trade unionism'. No precise form of measurement of the concept was proposed, but it was argued that 'a useful rough measure is obtained by considering the concept as comprising seven elements'. These are:

(i)   regarding collective bargaining and the protection of its members' interests as its main function;
(ii)   independence of employers;
(iii) militancy;
(iv)   declaring itself to be a trade union;
(v)   registration as a trade union;
(vi)   affiliation to the TUC;
(vii) affiliation to the Labour Party.

These seven items, some of which could not easily be measured individually, were thought to vary together to a substantial extent, but not so perfectly that any one of them taken alone could be regarded as a satisfactory measure of the concept. However it was suggested that the last four were somewhat different in being 'primarily measures of the level of identification with the labour movement' (Blackburn, 1967, 20). This point was not then developed, but later, in pursuing the theoretical and measurement problems, it was seen as desirable to separate out the aspect covered, broadly, by items (i) to (iii) from that covered by items (iv) to (vii). At a superficial level the problem that arises is that whereas there is a fairly marked tendency for these two aspects to vary together, so supporting the idea of conceptual unity, it is also possible to find examples both of associations which are, say, affiliated to the Labour Party but have a low degree of militancy and, more importantly in the non-manual field, of associations prepared to be highly militant but not rating highly on the second aspect.

   In attempting to deal with these problems of measurement it was clear that the solution lay in an extension of the original intention of conceptual clarification and of approaching the question from a theoretical perspective rather than by trying to generalise merely from the characteristics of particular types of organisations. The meaningful relation between the two aspects of unionateness could then be seen to derive from the fact that both reflect 'class' action, in that they are concerned with strategies for bringing about changes in the distribution of rewards. The distinction between them is a result of the fact that they relate to strategies within different distributional structures, or rather different aspects of the same structure. Thus we were led to a distinction between what we refer to as enterprise unionateness and society unionateness. The former concept refers to those aspects of the behaviour of an organisation which are concerned with the pursuit of the interests of its members as employees through collective action. Society unionateness covers those aspects of an organisation's character which concern its relation with other, similar organisations and its behaviour in the wider society.

Three points about the definition of enterprise unionateness need to be stressed. Firstly, we wish it to refer simply to a strategy for the pursuit of interests which are 'immediate' or 'instrumental' in Lockwood's terms (1958), and no connotation of ideological identification is intended. In this sense it is only one of a possible set of strategies available, all of which are means of pursuing group interests with regard to material conditions, job regulation and so on. Moreover, no assumption is made about the actual success of the strategy, but simply its nature as one. Secondly, the definition emphasises the important features of this particular strategy, that it relates to employees (and not, for example, to self-employed groups) and that it is collective. Therefore, the idea of behaviour of the organisation *vis-à-vis* one or more employees is intrinsic to the concept, and forms of action such as professionalism, for example (see Prandy, 1965a, 1965b), which may help strengthen the market position of members only as individuals are not included.

The third point is that in considering strategies we must necessarily take into account the behaviour of other parties. Since we have confined the application of the concept to employees it should be obvious that we recognise the importance of employers. Enterprise unionateness involves the idea of a progression of activities; an increasing assertion of the differences of interest between employer and employee and of the independence of the representative association, as well as the threat of increasingly severe sanctions to back up claims. Movement along such a continuum clearly depends on the employer's response, and not only on the employees' behaviour. One practical consequence of this is that in placing a particular association on the continuum the emphasis is less on its actual behaviour than on its willingness to countenance various activities. For example, the extent to which a particular trade union has to use the strike as a sanction in collective bargaining will be determined by a number of factors (such as the power of the employers) in the situation in which it finds itself. However, its acceptance of the strike as a possible sanction will be less dependent upon such immediate constraints, and related more to a wider range of experience. In many ways the situation here closely parallels that of the problem of the existence of attitudes at the individual level, and is if anything likely to be more complex. For example, there is a difficulty regarding the internal dynamics of an organisation, say whether one should take account in some general way of the attitudes of the organisation's members, or pay attention instead to those of the leadership, who may regard certain groups of members as constraints in the situation.

In considering the second of our concepts, that of society unionateness, there are fewer complexities. The reference to 'other, similar organisations' in our earlier definition implies that some degree of enterprise unionateness is a necessary, though not a sufficient, condition for a non-zero placement on the scale. Essentially, what the concept involves is a recognition by the organisation of the similarity of its interests to those of other organisations and a willingness to ally itself with them. More particularly, we are concerned with the extent of identification with the wider trade union movement. In part this may be instrumental, but in so far as the labour movement also has its political aspect then there are also involved what would normally be called ideological elements. In practice the distinction between instrumental and ideological is not at all clear, and one may choose to regard political action as in part just a longer-term strategy for the pursuit of group interests through, for example, policies aimed at redistribution of income or greater state control over industry. In this respect, therefore, society unionateness mirrors enterprise unionateness. The difference between them is that the former is of wider compass, both in that it is a strategy for action at the societal or political level, and in that it thereby involves alliance within a larger and more general interest grouping.

The reasons for anticipating a strong relationship between enterprise and society unionateness are clear enough, in that for the most part those pursuing collective strategies for a change in the distribution of rewards in the sphere of employment are likely to extend their activities into the political or societal sphere. For certain groups this arena may prove to be a more fruitful one for attaining their objectives. On the other hand some groups, particularly those who are relatively advantaged compared to other groups of employees, may well see little or nothing to gain from alliance with them. Indeed, in so far as ideological issues are involved, and where association with other groups may be seen as equating themselves with status and socio-economic inferiors, there may well be perceived losses.

These ideas relating to the concept of unionateness as an attribute of organisations can also be used as a basis for constructing measures of individual propensity, which are our present concern. This involves looking at individuals' desires regarding the behaviour of representative organisations. In order to discover both whether, and how, individuals perceive a unidimensional scale of society unionateness we presented our respondents with the following five items, asking them to indicate their degree of agreement or disagreement in five response categories:

(1) 'Most people need some sort of organisation to protect their interests with regard to their employment.'
(2) 'I would prefer to be in an internal company association rather than a trade union.'
(3) 'I would prefer to be in a registered trade union' (this was prior to the Industrial Relations Act which changed the significance of registration).
(4) 'I would prefer to be in an organisation affiliated to the TUC rather than one not affiliated.'
(5) 'I would prefer to be in an organisation affiliated to the Labour Party rather than one not affiliated.'

For the reasons described in the article previously referred to, we adopted the procedure of scoring the items from 1 to 5 and then simply adding the scores without any weighting.

Our measure of enterprise unionateness is based upon the application of Coombs' unfolding analysis and techniques related to it (Coombs, 1964). Briefly, we were able to scale respondents according to their ordering of, and thus in a sense their perceptions of their distance from, the following five statements, each of which is preceded by the clause 'People like me need, on our behalf':

A 'no kind of collective representation';
B 'a representative body to consult with and advise the employers on salaries and conditions';

C 'a representative body to negotiate with the employers';
D 'a representative body to negotiate, which is prepared, if necessary, to take mild industrial action';
E 'a representative body to negotiate which is prepared, if necessary, to take full strike action'.

Each step was intended to represent an advance, in terms of militancy and of independence from the employer, which might occur if the milder form fails to achieve the group's objectives which are concerned with salaries and conditions. The phrase 'representative body' was used so as to make it clear that internal staff associations were included as well as 'outside', trade-union type organisations. The introduction to the question was also meant to clarify this issue.

Each statement, with the first part repeated in each case, was set out on a separate card. The cards were handed to the respondent, in random order, and he was asked to put them in order from the one with which he most agreed to that with which he least agreed (or with which he most disagreed). The majority of respondents gave one of the eleven response patterns which constitute a compatible ordering of the five items, while the remainder were fitted on the basis of similarity, using multidimensional scaling. Responses were scored on a range from 0 to 66, with the scores for the compatible orderings as follows: ABCDE (0), BACDE (11), BCADE (17), BCDAE (26), BCDEA (31), CBDEA (32), CDBEA (43), DCBEA (47), DCEBA (51), DECBA (57) and EDCBA (66).

In considering the overall levels of society and enterprise unionateness it is useful to look also at the differences in scores between occupational groups in the total sample (Table 6.1). Since there were five items in the society unionateness scale and five response categories for each item, giving a possible range from 5 to 30, we can see that the overall mean falls a little below the middle category. Foremen, draughtsmen and clerks score slightly higher than this on average; professionals, managers and security men slightly lower. The differences between the groups are nonetheless very significant, somewhat more so than the differences in enterprise unionateness. In the latter case the overall mean, and those of the four highest-scoring groups – draughtsmen, clerks, technicians and foremen – are closest to only third of the 11 scale positions that we identified. This means the highest agreement is with the second item (a body to consult with and advise employers) and the next highest with the third (a body to negotiate). Greatest disagreement is with the two items suggesting the use of industrial action.

TABLE 6.1 *Mean enterprise and society unionateness scores by type of employment and occupational group (numbers in each cell in parentheses)*

Occupational group	Total sample		Private employment		Public employment	
	Enterprise	Society	Enterprise	Society	Enterprise	Society
Security	17.8 (16)	13.1 (16)	17.8 (16)	13.1 (16)	–	–
Foremen	26.4 (244)	15.9 (248)	26.4 (241)	15.8 (245)	25.7 (3)	17.3 (3)
Clerks	28.8 (612)	15.4 (617)	27.4 (491)	15.2 (492)	34.6 (121)	16.2 (125)
Draughtsmen	31.4 (80)	15.8 (80)	31.6 (73)	15.8 (73)	29.1 (7)	15.0 (7)
Technicians	27.2 (382)	14.9 (386)	25.9 (320)	14.8 (324)	34.0 (62)	15.3 (62)
Professionals	24.8 (311)	14.1 (314)	20.4 (210)	13.9 (212)	33.8 (101)	14.4 (102)
Managers	19.3 (253)	13.7 (257)	14.9 (197)	13.3 (199)	35.0 (56)	14.7 (58)
Total	26.3 (1898)	14.9 (1918)	24.5 (1548)	14.8 (1561)	34.2 (350)	15.3 (357)

E values:
(1) between occupations:
   (a) total sample: enterprise 0.20,   society 0.20
   (b) private employment: enterprise 0.27,   society 0.22
   (c) public employment: enterprise 0.08*, society 0.22
(2) between types of employment:
   (a) total: enterprise 0.22,   society 0.05†
   (b) clerks: enterprise 0.18,   society 0.11
   (c) managers: enterprise 0.48,   society 0.16

* Not significant at the 5 per cent level.
† Not significant at the 1 per cent level.

The fact that the ordering of the means for the occupational groups is broadly the same in both cases suggests that similar factors are likely to be at work. However it is worth noting that while foremen, the group with the highest proportion having moved from manual jobs, score highest on society unionateness, they come only fourth in enterprise unionateness. This fact should alert us to the possibility that to some extent at least there may be a degree of independent variation in the two forms.

There is a further indication of this if we take account of employment in the private or public sector. The greater development of collective bargaining in the latter is, as we would expect, strongly associated with differences in enterprise unionateness. However, this must not be interpreted as reflecting greater conflict with public employers. We have stressed earlier that unionateness does not measure conflict, but rather a succession of activities for non-success at a lower level which must, in part, be explained by employers' reactions.

In the case of society unionateness the situation is different. Public or private employment is not usually of great importance as the basis of common organisational interests on wider social issues, and apart from a tendency for experience of belonging to a representative organisation to elicit more sympathy for such organisations in general, there is unlikely to be a carry-over from differences in enterprise unionateness. Thus, although there is a significant difference in mean scores on society unionateness, the distinction is far less pronounced.

The significance of this last point is clear when we consider the various occupational groups within the two types of employment. In the public sector the employment situations of the occupational groups is very similar, and in consequence we find that there is no significant difference between their scores on enterprise unionateness. This contrasts with the private sector where the differences in scores are marked. There, as we would anticipate, managers and professionals have much lower scores than foremen and clerks. (Security men represent an interesting if not entirely unexpected deviant case.)

The net effect of the influence of employment and occupation on enterprise unionateness can best be seen by comparing clerks and managers. Clerks in the public sector do have scores higher than their counterparts in the private sector, but for managers the difference is much greater.

Differences between occupational groups within each sector are of more importance for society unionateness. The administrators and professionals of public enterprise are as much distinguished from their foremen and clerks as are the managers and professionals of private enterprise from their lower groups. In consequence, if we make a similar comparison between clerks in each sector and between managers in each sector, we find that this time the relationships are very similar and comparatively low.

Thus there is a general pattern, of variation in unionateness with the occupational hierarchy, to which there is one major exception. There is no significant difference in enterprise unionateness between occupational groups in the public sector, while the overall level is higher than for any single group in private employment. Hence this contrasts with the situation as regards society unionateness, where the general pattern entails little difference between the sectors.

Determinants of society unionateness

Since society unionateness measures attitudes within a wider social context, it might seem that it is anyway not particularly relevant to behaviour in the employing enterprise. Furthermore, it might be objected, following our own argument above, that it is not likely to be affected by the individual's employment experience as much as by his general position within society. However, it is necessary to bear in mind that the individual's location within the employment structure is a very significant aspect of his place in society. Putting this another way, to make clearer the relevance to the present discussion, it is far too narrow a conception of employment situation to see it simply within the enterprise, apart from its location in the more general processes of the society. The variables and frames of reference already considered bear testimony to this, if any be needed. Therefore, the worker's commitment to, or alienation from, his present situation cannot be isolated from the attitudes measured here.

However we do find, when we look at the determinants of society unionateness (Table 6.2), that to a greater extent than for the strategies with which we dealt in the previous chapter, non-immediate work factors appear to predominate. The most important, both in public and private employment, which are shown separately, is whether the respondent's father was himself a member of a trade union. This demonstrates the importance of social origins in developing identification with the wider labour movement; not so much the fact of coming from a manual or a non-manual background,

TABLE 6.2   *Influences on society unionateness (path coefficients)*

(a) Private employment

Father non-manual	Father in trade union	Type of school	Part-time (day) further education	Distance moved	Years of service	Superiors: time	Present job status	Society status	Desired status	'Better opportunities'	Satisfaction with income	Residual
-0.08	0.16	-0.09	-0.06	0.06	0.09	-0.08	-0.06	-0.04	-0.09	0.06	-0.07	0.93

(b) Public employment

Father in trade union	Full-time further education	Part-time (day) further education	Attendance at political associations	Subordinates: number	Manual worker's income	Residual
0.22	-0.18	-0.12	-0.11	-0.13	-0.11	0.93

though this in itself is also significant for those employed in the private sector, as of acquiring attitudes generally favourable to trade unionism. Even then there is evidence that those anticipating higher status through going to a selective school or having further education, are less likely to retain such attitudes. Certainly they are less likely to hold them now.

Work-related factors tend to be more important for those employed in the private sector. There is a tendency for longer-service employees to have a higher level of society unionateness, and since these, as we have seen, tend to be better paid, it is important to stress that this effect operates together with a direct, negative one from satisfaction with income. The fact that it is the relatively lower-paid amongst the longer-service workers who tend to be more unionate shows up when satisfactions are excluded. In fact they appear to be those workers who also spend less time with their supervisors, who see themselves as being of lower status, and who have lower expectations regarding their social standing.

There are fewer significant determinants of society unionateness in the case of public employees. Those in positions of greater authority, at least in so far as this is indicated by the amount of time spent with subordinates, tend to be less unionate, as also do those who have higher perceptions of the earnings of manual workers. In the latter case it may well be that the effect runs in the opposite direction, so that those higher on society unionateness believe that manual workers have lower earnings, but at least it is clear that manual workers do not serve as a significant comparative reference group in fostering unionateness.

Finally, in this group, there is a negative effect from attendance at political meetings which presumably results from there being a number of respondents with a comparatively high level of involvement in the Conservative Party, who are strongly against close links between the trade union movement and the Labour Party.

Determinants of enterprise unionateness

When we turn to the determinants of enterprise unionateness (Table 6.3) we find that various aspects of income are the major influences, for both the privately and publicly employed. The importance of the aspects of income can be contrasted with the absence of any effect from total satisfaction, once again pointing to the limitations of the latter as a measure of the individual's commitment to the

TABLE 6.3 *Influences on enterprise unionateness (path coefficients)*

(a) Private employment

Father non-manual	Father in trade union	First job status	Service in firm	Superiors: time	Own level income	Top manager's income	Security: own level	Company status	Society status	Control	Security expectations	Satisfaction			Residual
												Income	Security	Superior	
−0.09	0.08	−0.08	0.07	−0.06	−0.11	0.10	−0.07	−0.05	−0.08	−0.06	0.08	−0.10	0.08	0.06	0.92

(b) Public employment

Father in trade union	Manual worker's income	Security: top manager	'Opportunities outside'	Satisfaction with income	Residual
0.12	−0.15	0.13	−0.19	−0.21	0.94

organisation. There is a strong tendency for greater militancy to be associated with dissatisfaction with earnings, particularly for those in public employment, while in private employment this is coupled with a direct influence from the respondent's assessment of the earnings of people like himself. As with society unionateness there is no indication that unfavourable comparisons with the earnings of manual workers lead to white-collar workers becoming more militant in response to a perceived threat; indeed the reverse is the case in public employment, while in the private sector there is an indication that top managers do serve as a reference group. One could argue that the comparison upward is more important, so that inequalities of income lead to increased unionateness where the salient reference group is one with whom the individual is at a disadvantage. Alternatively, it may be that at least to some extent the causal influence goes in the other direction and that those higher on unionateness tend to elevate the earnings of managers. However, if this were so we would have expected a similar result in the case of society unionateness. There may also be a contextual effect, such that in those establishments where there is a higher level of unionateness generally among non-manual workers, it is in fact the case that top management earns more.

Apart from income, the main influences on enterprise unionateness relate to security. In the public sector this only involves perceptions in relation to top management, but in private employment expectations and satisfaction are all significant. Higher unionateness is found among those who believe that they have less security than others doing a similar job to themselves and among those with higher expectations. Allowing for these two effects, though, it is found also amongst those who are more satisfied.

It is interesting to note that these economic variables, which are the major influences on enterprise unionateness, have much less effect on society unionateness; as we saw earlier (Table 6.2) income is much less important and security has no significant effects at all on the latter. However, most of the other influences here are relevant to both aspects of unionateness. In the private sector variables relating to status are rather more important. Those who see themselves as having lower social standing, in both the company and the wider society, are again more unionate, as also are those who began their working lives in lower-status jobs. Unionateness is associated with length of service, little contact with superiors, and in this case dissatisfaction with superiors as well. Also there are some remaining effects from social background. The sons of manual workers are more unionate, and so are those whose fathers were themselves members of a union. This last is again even more true of employees in the public sector, though in both cases the influence is much greater on society unionateness. Among public employees enterprise unionateness is also influenced by a belief in there being good opportunities outside the respondent's present employment.

The latter suggests that those individuals who see favourable prospects elsewhere are likely to be less committed to public employment generally, and in particular to its more extensive arrangements for respresentation. For the most part, though, we have further evidence that in this sector enterprise unionateness does not vary to any great extent by hierarchical position and associated rewards. Much more than in private employment it is seen at all levels as an appropriate response to a situation of dissatisfaction with income, and is one which tends to be followed instead of the more individual adaptations.

So far we have treated society and enterprise unionateness as separately determined variables, although we would expect that each of them tends to have an effect on the other and that both to some extent reflect a certain underlying unity. However, we have argued that to some extent this is true of all the adaptations, so we shall examine this question in the context of a more general model linking the different outcomes.

COMMITMENT TO THE ORGANISATION

Having looked at the determinants of each adaptation in isolation we can consider the question of whether or not these separate measures reflect an underlying degree of commitment to the employing organisation. There are two ways in which we might approach this problem. The first is to hypothesise the existence of a variable, commitment, which we have not been able to measure directly, but which could be taken as a cause of each of the individual outcomes. Thus we might argue that the relationships between each of these outcomes and its determinants are mediated through this hypothetical variable. We could relax this assumption a little, by allowing each particular indicator to be affected in part directly, as well as through the hypothetical variable.

The other way of considering the problem is to do away with the idea of an unmeasured concept, and instead to look at the way in which the different outcomes are influenced by one another, as well as by those factors which we have already seen to be determinants. That is, one might see them as alternative, or in some cases perhaps complementary, forms of behaviour, which can be looked at simply in terms of the measures themselves.

One way of taking the first approach is to use the method of canonical correlation, at least as it has been modified by Hauser and Goldberger (1971). This method, of modified generalised least-squares, enables one to consider all the determinants of a set of dependent variables as operating through an unmeasured variable. We can see how this works, first, in the particular case of the set of all the individual satisfactions as determinants of the set of outcomes including, for the present, total satisfaction. As we have already pointed out, it is not entirely clear to what extent we should regard total satisfaction as a consequence or a cause of commitment, but at this point it is more useful to treat it as the former.

The results are shown in Table 6.4. Looking first at the paths to the hypothetical variable from the independent variables, the satisfactions, we can see that their relative influences are much the same as when we considered total satisfaction alone. By far the most important is once again satisfaction with intrinsic job followed by satisfaction with promotion. At some distance come satisfaction with income and with social interaction. In keeping with this it is hardly surprising that the largest of the paths to the dependent variables is

TABLE 6.4 *Relations to a hypothetical variable of satisfaction*

Paths from independent variables

			Satisfaction			
Intrinsic job	Promotion	Income	Social interaction	Status	Security	Superior
0.46	0.35	0.16	0.14	0.10	0.09	0.09

Paths to dependent variables

Total satisfaction	Job attachment	Attitude to management	Self-estrangement	Enterprise unionateness	Society unionateness
0.79	0.64	0.49	−0.44	−0.17	−0.07

Canonical correlation: 0.82

that to total satisfaction. However, job attachment also has a strong relationship, as also does attitude to top management and, to a lesser extent, self-estrangement. The unionateness items, especially society unionateness, appear not to be very well related to the hypothetical variable.

It is clear that the unmeasured variable in this case is basically related to satisfaction, and although perhaps an improvement on total satisfaction taken alone it can only be regarded as a partial indicator of commitment. For each of the personal adaptations we found that rewards and perceptions continued to act independently of satisfaction. We can expect to get a better measure, therefore, if we look at a rather larger and broader set of independent variables made up of all those factors which have been shown to be significant individually on any of the dependent variables. In doing this we can also cease to treat total satisfaction as one of the indicators of attachment, and instead include it amongst the causes. The results for this model are shown in Table 6.5. Furthermore, since we have seen that the outcomes are differently determined in the public as compared to the private sector, we shall present separate analyses for the two types of employment.

Total satisfaction now becomes the most important determinant of the hypothetical variable of commitment for both the publicly and privately employed. Among the latter group the only individual satisfactions that remain of any significance are security and income, while among the former the only one is satisfaction with superior. In fact its effect in their case is negative, serving to offset in part a strong positive influence from the associated perceptions. Several other perceptions have an additional effect even though they are well correlated with total satisfaction. Considering both groups together, the most important are use of abilities, promotion and, to a lesser extent, company status and social interaction. It is interesting that it is in the public sector with its more formalised salary structure that there is to be found the pattern of opposing influences of the individual's own earnings and his perceptions of what is earned by those like himself. As at a number of previous points in our analysis we find that there is a high level of identification with the occupational group. Also in the public sector we find that the positive effect of use of abilities is partly offset by a negative influence from intrinsic job expectations. No such pattern is found in the private sector where, indeed, the only contribution from expectations is from those of promotion. Here higher expectations are related to stronger commitment; we have generally assumed that expectations help determine commitment, but how far the assumption is justified in this case we shall examine shortly.

Overall, then, it is clear that those who enjoy higher rewards, in part in so far as this is reflected in higher levels of satisfaction, are more strongly committed to the organisation. Once again, however, we find that, allowing for these influences, age is still important, with older respondents in the private sector, and less markedly longer-service employees in the public sector, exhibiting a greater degree of commitment.

For the outcomes, apart from our omission of total satisfaction, the results are similar to those found for the earlier model. Job attachment, attitude to top management and self-estrangement are again quite strongly related to the hypothetical construct. Amongst those in private employment, bringing in the wider set of independent variables does show an increase in the relationship of the hypothetical variable to the two unionateness items, but as before, and especially for society unionateness, they are much lower than for other outcomes. Part, but certainly not all, of the increase is a result of separating out those in the public sector. Here the relationships are very weak, as we would anticipate, given the very high level of institutionalisation of collective bargaining. In both sectors we are led to the conclusion that unionateness is not as clearly related to commitment as are the other indicators.

However, as we said earlier there is another way of considering the inter-relationships between the outcomes of commitment. This does not postulate the existence of an underlying concept, but rather involves seeing the extent to which these variables interact with one another. Whereas the previous model is based on the assumption that each indicator reflects the hypothetical variable, and that any one of them is a possible outcome of it, this alternative puts more emphasis on the way in which the variables influence one another. In particular it is an attempt to allow for the possibility that forms of experience, even though they arise from similar conditions, are exclusive rather than complementary. To some extent at least following one course tends to lead to a neglect of the others. Thus, although they may still be related to one another conceptually, this may not be entirely reflected empirically, since the positive relationship deriving from their common determination may be offset by the negative relationship from each to the others.

In looking at this model we shall introduce a further change by

TABLE 6.5 Relations to a hypothetical variable of commitment

(a) Private employment
Major paths from independent variables

Total satisfaction	Age	Use of abilities	Promotion perceptions	Satisfaction with income	Satisfaction with security	Company status	Promotion expectations
0.39	0.25	0.22	0.20	0.12	0.11	0.10	0.10

Paths to dependent variables

Job attachment	Attitude to management	Self-estrangement	Enterprise unionateness	Society unionateness
0.73	0.56	−0.50	−0.24	−0.12

Canonical correlation: 0.77

(b) Public employment
Major paths from independent variables

Total satisfaction	Own level earnings (company)	Income	Use of abilities	Perceptions of superior	Intrinsic job expectations	Promotion perceptions	Satisfaction with superior	Social interaction perceptions	Service in firm
0.65	0.53	−0.49	0.27	0.23	−0.16	0.12	−0.11	0.11	0.10

Paths to dependent variables

Job attachment	Self-estrangement	Attitude to management	Enterprise unionateness	Society unionateness
0.76	−0.63	0.58	−0.03	−0.02

Canonical correlation: 0.83

including promotion amongst the outcomes. We have so far included it amongst the rewards, though referring at various points to its ambiguous nature. However, given the importance of promotion as a means of changing current conditions it is clearly much more necessary in this model to treat it in a similar way to the other outcomes. This adds a further complication to an already complex model in which each outcome potentially determines all of the others. Ideally one would like to study this as a process, using data collected over a period of time. When data collected at a single point in time are used, not only is the element of process necessarily missing, but one is faced with an additional technical problem. Because the variables determine one another, the residual in the regression for each is correlated with the other. The method of two-stage least-squares that we adopt overcomes this problem to a reasonable extent by replacing the actual value of any endogenous variable (that is, one being explained) with an estimated value derived from an ordinary regression on all the independent exogenous variables, whenever that variable is included amongst the determinants of another (Duncan, Haller and Portes, 1968; Johnston, 1963, ch. 9).

Further, we need to simplify the model as much as possible, partly in order not to be overwhelmed by the inter-relationships, but more importantly, so as to be able to see whether a simple set of relationships are sufficient to represent the dynamics of the situation. Thus we have tried successive models, eliminating non-significant paths.

The basic models that are suggested by our analysis are shown in Figures 6.1 and 6.2. Taking the private sector first, what is immediately clear is the correctness of including expectations of promotion amongst the outcomes, for we can see that this particular strategy is dependent upon several of the others. First, however, we should note that it is itself a determinant only of satisfaction with promotion, which in turn determines job attachment and total satisfaction. The relationship of this last to the other elements of the model is an interesting one, in so far as it is the only one which is simply dependent. This reinforces earlier doubts about its ambiguous status, indicating that it is strictly an outcome of the individual's situation but not linked to the other outcomes.

It is job attachment which holds the central position among the adaptations. The greater it is, the more favourable is the individual's attitude towards top management, and the lower are his self-estrangement and expectations of promotion. Job attachment, that is to say, appears to be a primary indicator of the outcomes. Low attachment

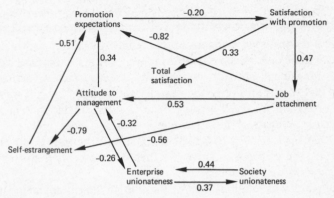

FIGURE 6.1   *Schematic diagram of inter-relationships of outcomes: private sector*

then leads on to each of the others – to higher expectations of promotion, a greater degree of self-estrangement or, indirectly, a higher level of enterprise unionateness.

This last link is through attitude to top management, and it is the only one between unionateness and the other strategies. Where the attitude is more favourable, enterprise unionateness tends to be lower, and this is accompanied by a reciprocal effect, such that higher unionateness leads to a less favourable attitude. Consistent with the earlier findings regarding society unionateness, that it was much less affected than other factors by the immediate work situation, is the fact that it has the least direct link to the remaining outcomes; its connection is solely through enterprise unionateness. It seems clear that society unionateness is more the result of wider social influences which it channels to influence enterprise unionateness than the result of experience in the immediate work situation. There are reciprocal effects tending to bring the two types of unionateness into closer alignment. This supports the conceptualisation of two different but related aspects, rather than totally distinct variables.

The position of attitude to top management in the model is almost on a par with that of job attachment. Apart from the link to enterprise unionateness, it has an influence on two other adaptations. As with job attachment, where there is a more favourable attitude towards management there is also likely to be a lower degree of self-estrangement and a higher level of expectations of promotion. This last effect in part offsets the more direct one from job attachment, as also do the indirect influences through self-estrangement. That is to say, those higher on self-estrangement tend to have lower expectations.

There is thus good evidence in this model of the way in which the emergence of one outcome tends to inhibit others. In particular both self-estrangement and job attachment, directly, have a depressive effect on expectations of promotion. By a less direct route, if we trace the connections from self-estrangement to enterprise unionateness the net effect is again a negative one – that is, those high on self-estrangement are likely to be less unionate. In the reverse direction, however, the effect is positive, so that the more unionate tend to become more self-estranged.

The pattern of relationships for those in public employment shares certain similarities with that for the private sector, but it is not identical, as we would expect given the different determinants of the various outcomes. Perhaps the first point to note is that the two aspects of unionateness are not involved with the other factors in the public sector. The earlier model of a hypothetical variable of commitment indicated that neither of them was at all well related to the other outcomes, and the present analysis confirms this. Widespread collective bargaining, as an *institutional* feature, is clearly not related to these other, more individualistic, adaptations. Because of this the relationship between the two types of unionateness is also different from that in the private sector. While society unionateness has no influence upon the enterprise aspect, there is a moderate effect in the reverse direction, reflecting a tendency for greater sympathy for the general trade union movement among those who are more involved in their own organisation.

There are other respects in which the models for the two sectors are very different. Neither self-estrangement nor attitude to top management have any significant influence upon promotion expectations, while the effect from job attachment to self-estrangement is replaced by one in the opposite direction. However, one effect – the negative one from attitude to top management to self-estrangement – persists unchanged, and others are variations on a basically similar pattern. These are the ones involving the two satisfactions. In the public sector, satisfaction with promotion is purely dependent upon promotion expectations, and does not in its turn influence any other outcome, even total satisfaction. One consequence of this is that there is now a direct effect from promotion expectations to job attachment. Total satisfaction, by contrast, assumes a more central importance. Influences that in the private

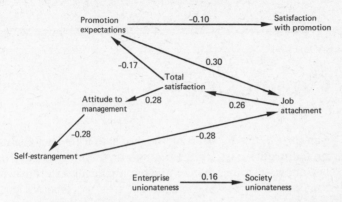

FIGURE 6.2 *Schematic diagram of inter-relationships of outcomes: public sector*

sector model go directly to promotion expectations and attitude to management are instead mediated through total satisfaction.

In comparing the two types of models that we have presented from a theoretical point of view, and failing a model which would in some way combine the two approaches, there is much to be said for the second. Its assumptions are less simple and it allows for more complex relationships. In particular it demonstrates more clearly the dynamics of the relationships between adaptations. However it is worth noting the similarities between the two models, particularly for those in private employment. Amongst the latter, job attachment and attitude towards top management were the two major indicators of commitment in the simpler model; in the more complex one the same two variables occupied a central position, with job attachment as a determinant of three other individual outcomes, and with attitudes towards top management mediating between the latter and a collective strategy.

7 Conclusions

We began this volume by asserting the fascination for sociologists of studying the middle class. In presenting our findings we have dealt with class implicitly rather than setting our arguments centrally within a class model. It is now incumbent upon us to elaborate on the relationship between our approach and traditional class analysis.

SUMMARY

In order to do this we shall first try to summarise some of the salient results of our research in the context of a discussion of the general model that we have used, which was described in the first chapter. Very briefly, in that model the interaction of rewards, perceptions and expectations is seen as leading, under different sets of conditions, to various outcomes and adaptations, either individual or collective, to the rewards and costs of employment. We tried in Chapter 1 to give an account of the position from which we started, rather than reinterpret it to be compatible with our conclusions and our later ideas. Although we would still regard that model as useful, we would hold that it needs developing to produce a more adequate treatment of the links between the processes included within it and the wider social system. In broad terms, this involves reinterpreting individual action as part of the social process.

One weakness in our model is that, although it is centrally concerned with the distribution of rewards, it tends to take the existence of the rewards as a starting point, and thus to neglect the processes by which they are produced and maintained. The generation of the distribution of rewards clearly involves much wider issues than can be dealt with directly in a research project of this kind. For the most part distribution is considered simply in relation to the way in which individuals possessing particular characteristics come to enjoy different levels of rewards. Of course this was never intended to imply that the individual characteristics necessarily determine these levels; in the case of intrinsic job rewards and security, in particular, it is quite clear that the levels are primarily determined by more general processes of the social system. The case of earnings is more arguable, and is one to which we shall return in discussing the relation of market forces to social class.

A second respect in which more general social processes are neglected derived from certain elements of a social action approach which remain in our analysis. Because the original formulation tended to be couched at the level of individual action, there is inevitably a particular theoretical emphasis in the subsequent account. Thus, despite our efforts to criticise the social action approach, the emphasis on perceptions, expectations, satisfactions and adaptations would appear to lie firmly within it. However, though this has placed emphasis upon the individual it was never intended to separate him from social circumstances, and we noted when discussing psychological withdrawal that there were always implicit in the theoretical scheme certain ideas which became more explicit in the course of the research. The point is not that we wish to deny that behaviour varies, but rather that it must be understood in context. The model goes some way towards this, as it must since it contains collective action, arising out of common circumstances, as a major element. Nonetheless, collective action is still taken as a means of pursuing individual interests, albeit shared ones, and though this may be the way in which it is understood by those involved, such an understanding is only partial. It is also necessary to appreciate how such individual understandings relate to a wider social system both in the sense that behaviour is facilitated and constrained by relationships with other aspects of the system and in the sense that the understandings contribute to its maintenance or change.

The relationship of individual experience to social processes is far from straightforward. At first glance promotion might appear to be an individual experience, and at the level of personal understanding this may be the case, but in truth the distribution of opportunities and the criteria for their realisation are part of a reproducing system. On the other hand collective action may appear, since it is social in nature, to be external to the individual and constraining upon him. However, our argument is that in some of its aspects collective action is a denial of existing social determinants, and the means by which individuals, collectively, can contribute to the realisation of objectives not embedded in current understandings and experiences. The separation of the 'individual' from the 'social' is ultimately false.

In general, understandings of social processes are conditioned by the particular nature of experiences of individuals and groups in definite relations to each other in social systems. Such understandings may be limited and partial, but in so far as they are adequate to the purposes of behaviour they are the means by which social systems are reproduced. Facilities for and constraints upon individual and group behaviour are at one and the same time cognitive and practical. On most occasions practical understandings are undermined and transformed in only the most marginal manner. Individuals and groups are concerned with small variations of understandings and circumstances and, though such variations may lead on to more fundamental change, for the most part they are associated with attempts to redress minor imbalances or consolidate small gains.

The rigid nature of cognitive constraints is very clearly demonstrated in our results in the case of expectations. What emerges from our analyses of these is that the great majority of our respondents are, with regard to the levels of rewards that they think they ought to get, highly constrained by the levels that they are actually getting. What differences do exist seem to derive, as we are able to show in the case of income, from a belief that others whom they consider to be much like themselves are receiving more than they are, and not as a result of comparisons with other groups differently located. Thus, for example, our non-manual respondents do not seem to be much concerned about the earnings of manual workers in deciding what they themselves ought to be earning, and neither do most of them bother about the upward comparison with top managers. This is not to say that they are unaware of the earnings of these other groups, since the average figure given for manual workers is quite clearly below, and that for top managers above, that for their own occupational group. It is not, therefore, ignorance of the structure of income inequalities which prevents comparison, but the fact that such comparison is not of great salience. The existence of inequality is taken as intrinsic to the operation of the system.

However, if the nature of preferred experience varies little from actual experience in terms of the system as whole, this does not imply that the variations are of little consequence for individuals and groups. The most important emotional issues in employment situations occur in relation to just such marginal variations in experience. Being passed over for promotion or seeing differentials eroded are major sources of disaffection with management and the company because these are issues over which individual managements are seen to have control. This has two consequences. The first is that the management can be held responsible for the variations, and the second is the related point that since managements are regarded as competent to exercise control they can be pressurised to change the situation. In those circumstances where managements are competent, workers are also potentially competent. In terms of wider issues of the operation of the system neither are judged to be competent; for example, individual managements do not create the capitalist system and to survive they must work within it, while senior government officials are not held directly responsible for basic departmental objectives and conditions of employment.

Social circumstances and individual adaptations

What we have referred to as 'adaptations' stand in differing relations to the reproduction of the society. Some are best seen as features of a stable reproducing system while others are concerned with disruptions of processes, whether the concern is to produce novel advantages or redress the disadvantages of previous disruption. Promotion falls firmly in the former category. Our results strongly suggest that there is a good deal of predictable regularity about the process of attainment. As we have argued elsewhere in developing this point (Stewart, Prandy and Blackburn, 1980) it is theoretically more plausible to see the process as itself an aspect of the system. Promotion occurs within social processes which are sufficiently predictable to raise doubts about the degree of effective decision-making that is possible. However, its special characteristic is that it allows just such a sense of personal choice and voluntarism within a stable system. This sense of competence is an important aspect of the experience of non-manual workers (cf. Kohn, 1969), which of course is reinforced by the very predictability of the process. As we have argued, the emphasis on individual attainment tends to deflect concern away from the system itself and so also from ways of attempting to change it. As an individual strategy, therefore, career advancement helps to maintain and reproduce the existing system.

There is considerable evidence in our results of the part played by promotion. For example, those with more favourable perceptions of their chances of advancement tend to have lower expectations with respect to the other rewards attaching to their present position. In some cases, even allowing for the effect of these lower expectations, they are also more satisfied with those rewards. For some this is because of promotion actually experienced, and thus an acceptance of personal attainment as satisfactory; for others it is because high expectations of promotion lead them to believe in future improvement in their position. This last is demonstrated more clearly in the influence that higher expectations of promotion have in increasing the level of satisfaction with other rewards.

If, as we have been arguing, promotion prospects are generally stable and predictable we would expect that disruptions of expectations would have considerable negative effects upon attitudes towards managements and in certain circumstances encourage an approving attitude towards militancy. In fact, our findings show that a perceived lack of promotion opportunities is the major factor in the development of a critical attitude towards top management. In turn negative attitudes to management are the major determinants of support for collective responses. Thus enterprise unionateness is encouraged where the company's management are held responsible for unsatisfactory features.

To this extent there is some validity in the argument that a decline in promotion opportunities leads to the 'proletarianisation' of white-collar workers. However, such arguments for the most part wrongly identify the processes occurring. The form of unionism encouraged is specific and depends upon a 'non-proletarian' identity. Furthermore, as we have argued elsewhere (Stewart, Prandy and Blackburn, 1980), there is no convincing evidence of any decline in men's opportunities for promotion over a considerable time period. The present study has provided very clear evidence of the significance of personal advancement – or at least of career structures which are seen as such, and certainly, whatever may be the overall trend, particular individuals have not suffered a decline. It is more likely that those lower-level positions with lower chances for advancement are in fact filled by ex-manual workers.

Moreover, our evidence suggests that blocked promotion is also associated with the development of self-estrangement, an individualistic form of avoidance through psychological withdrawal from the situation. This, together with job attachment, is another adaptation associated with stable processes of reproduction. Job attachment has two aspects. In the first place attachment is negatively related to promotion expectations, and if this were the only process low levels of attachment would be unlikely to reflect low commitment to the system as a whole. Secondly, however, and more importantly, low job attachment is related to low levels of intrinsic job rewards and this is even more true for psychological withdrawal. Those with less varied jobs, offering less scope for individual control, are less attached to their jobs and also have higher levels of psychological withdrawal. Once again, however, it is difficult to explain the process in terms of deliberate individual 'strategies'. As outcomes, low levels of commitment to employment and high levels of self-estrangement are more intelligible as aspects of social processes than as conscious and competent individual behaviours chosen in relation to judgements of social circumstances.

To some extent, in both of these cases, it may be that some individuals do consciously decide to make only a reduced commitment to work. This seems most likely to be the case with job attachment, where in part our measure was one of desire for permanent withdrawal from the situation by taking a job elsewhere. Of course, even this is constrained, as is shown by the greater job attachment of older workers, whose opportunities for alternative employment are limited. Furthermore, the fact that the least varied and interesting jobs brought forth the lowest attachment suggests a direct link, that is that such jobs were intrinsically less involving.

The role of consciousness is even more problematic in the case of psychological withdrawal. Here again, a deliberate decision to act out a role is not impossible, but given the nature of the measure that we used it seems unlikely that any more than a small minority of higher scores arise from a process of that kind. For the majority, psychological withdrawal is not a strategy which is consciously pursued, although in so far as it involves giving to the employer no more of self than the minimum it may be no less rational for that. Thus it can be seen as behaviour which is an outcome of the individual's situation, rather than a conscious strategy. From the individual's point of view there may appear to be only limited opportunity for decision-making, especially since his understanding of his situation will be constrained by his experience, and thus by his social location. Psychological withdrawal is only an extreme, or very clear, illustration of this, where the form of understanding of the situation is itself a part of the adaptation.

Satisfaction with intrinsic job rewards is the major determinant of total job satisfaction and the actual levels of rewards also have direct effects, yet dissatisfaction is not related to approval of collective action. As with the argument about 'declining promotion opportunities', it is not clear whether the process of 'deskilling' is supposed to affect individuals on any scale. Our data do not enable us to look at that question, but what we can say is that although those who hold the least varied and most constrained jobs experience them as depriving, their sense of self-estrangement and non-commitment does not encourage any move towards organised protest. The general structure of employment is not seen as susceptible to change through collective action, and as individuals grow older without personal improvement in their conditions they develop a fatalistic attitude to their position. Deprivation does not, of itself, lead to radical action. In fact those most deprived are probably least likely to hold understandings which include the efficacy of personal action to relieve deprivation (cf. Prandy, 1979).

To a large extent, then, low levels of job attachment and high levels of self-estrangement are a consequence of occupying lowly positions in the occupational hierarchy. They reflect a helplessness and hopelessness about changing the characteristics of these positions. However, it seems likely, given the strong relationship of satisfaction with intrinsic job and total satisfaction with job attachment and self-estrangement, that not all of the effect is from expected features of employment. We have, after all, argued that to some extent satisfaction is determined by variations from expectations rather than by feelings of contentment or discontentment. In that case it would result from the disruption of regular social processes rather than directly from their character. On the evidence available it seems likely that satisfaction with intrinsic aspects of the job varies both with standard processes and with their disruption. To some extent judgement is of work as against other areas of experience and this can reflect standard processes, while to some extent judgement is of deviations from expectation of intrinsic job rewards. What is clear, however, is that dissatisfaction with intrinsic rewards does not give rise to strongly unfavourable attitudes to management and a desire for collective organisation. It may be that deviations from expectations in this area are seen to be chiefly a consequence of changes in, or unexpected features of, technical job requirements over which managements have little control. In addition senior employees who are dissatisfied with intrinsic aspects of their job are unlikely to see collective action as the means of alleviating the situation. What is clear is that in whatever way the deviation from expectations arise, they do not favour organised protest.

Both as accommodations to what are viewed as standard social processes and as responses to deprivations suffered in the disruption of expectations, low job attachment and high self-estrangement contribute to the reproduction of the conditions of deprivation.

The adaptation which is most clearly associated with extended reproduction and change in the conditions of deprivation is expressing some desire for collective representation. In so far as we treat support for collective bargaining simply as a strategy by which the individual might expect to increase or maintain his own income we necessarily neglect its importance as a means of protecting those employees who would most suffer under 'free market' conditions. Nonetheless the fact of concerted action, however narrowly defined the interests, is in itself of considerable significance in indicating a movement away from individualistically conceived interests. Moreover we have distinguished between the pursuit of interests within the framework of the employing enterprise and wider identification with the labour movement. The strength of the relationship between these depends on the location of the particular group within the employing enterprise and in the total society. Thus conditions in the former may be conducive to the development of collective bargaining for a group which holds a relatively privileged position within the wider society, and in these circumstances the level of society unionateness is likely to be lower, however high the level of enterprise unionateness. A good example of this is the case of those in professional and managerial positions in public employment. While their level of enterprise unionateness is not significantly different from that of those in lower-level employment, their level of society unionateness is considerably lower and not very different from that of people similar to themselves in the private sector.

Of course in situations where, as in public employment, collective representation is well established it is less clear that we are dealing with extended reproduction rather than with the stable reproduction of a changed circumstance. However, we have to take account not only of the fact that a change has occurred, but that presumably without a continued commitment there would be a reversion to the previous situation. The fact that in the public sector greater militancy is associated more with personal dissatisfaction with earnings than with hierarchical position suggests that change in the structure of rewards is less likely in future, and it may be the case that such situations come to be defined as normal. Nevertheless, there may also be consequences which extend beyond the immediate situation of employment, and which constitute one aspect of a more long-term process. This is a large question that we cannot deal with here, related as it is to the more general issue of how extensive is the change that unionateness, when translated into actual collective representation, serves to bring about.

For the most part, however, our results suggest that the desire for some form, albeit usually a mild one, of collective representation is more widespread than is the practice. There would thus seem to be the potential for future development. We have already referred in this section to the fact that a favourable attitude towards collective representation is fostered under circumstances where managements are held responsible for undesirable features of experience. Unless this occurs, then, to use a major example, poor promotion prospects will lead only to a more individualistic adaptation. While we were doubtful about the idea of proletarianisation as referring to a process, for the individual, of declining opportunities for promotion and deskilling, we would not wish to deny that among non-manual workers the desire for collective representation is more developed in situations less differentiated from those of manual workers, and to that extent proletarian. As we have shown, social location, as indicated by income, perceived status and previous occupation, is an important determinant of enterprise unionateness. Those who are themselves of manual-worker origin, who are in the least well-paid, lower-status jobs are the most likely to favour collective bargaining. The significance of such factors clearly illustrates the role of interests in encouraging collective action, and its socially located nature. The fact that the more subjective aspects, expectations and satisfactions, were less obviously involved in part results not from their inapplicability in this particular outcome, but from their relationship, particularly among those in more favoured positions, with various other more likely adaptations.

Nonetheless, in looking at society unionateness it is clear that what is important is social experience in a very broad sense, particularly the individual's social origins. Being brought up in a manual-worker home and having a father who had himself been a member of a trade union are major influences on the degree of identification with the wider labour movement, independently of factors concerned with the respondent's present employment. It appears also that the influence of society unionateness upon enterprise unionateness is somewhat greater than that in the reverse direction. Certainly, therefore, social class background and broader identification with the labour movement must be taken into account.

It is at this point that our concern with unionateness, as one of a number of possible adaptations, merges into the more usual concern with class action. There is an objection that taking identification with the labour movement, society unionateness, as an indicator of class consciousness ties the latter too closely to trade unions. This is seen as a social democratic bias which ignores other, more genuinely revolutionary, manifestations of class consciousness. Such a criticism gains some strength in the context of Britain, where the labour movement has for the most part avoided revolutionary political action. However this fact also points to its weakness, for except from an extreme left-wing position it would be difficult to classify the labour movements of France and Italy, for example, as social democratic. More basically, the question that is raised here is about the meaning and nature of class consciousness. If this is to be defined in a narrow way, as relating only to revolutionary consciousness, then one is clearly left, in the British context, with a concept of very limited utility. In other situations one might need indicators of society unionateness which were more closely related to revolutionary consciousness, but it would be a mistake to confuse the indicators, which are necessary for an empirical test of a theory, with the concepts to which they relate. However, we would go beyond this, and argue that the emphasis on class *consciousness* is misplaced. As we have tried to show, the emphasis needs to be placed, instead, on behaviour, and on the way in which it serves to reproduce or to change existing social arrangements, in particular those usually subsumed under the label of class.

MARKET PRINCIPLES, CLASS AND SOCIAL REPRODUCTION

A major difficulty in class analysis has been to provide an account of social systems, including social classes, which also explains how the actions of individuals serve to reproduce these systems, perhaps with adaptations. While Marxism does attempt such an account, at least as regards the bourgeoisie and proletariat, it has suffered from an inability to deal theoretically with those groups which do not fit simply into one or other of its two major classes. Hence there have been a number of attempts by Marxist writers to delineate more closely the various groupings within the middle class, loosely defined. One basis has been that of a more refined economic identification (e.g. Carchedi, 1975; Wright, 1976, 1978, 1979), but this tends not even to attempt to explain the relationship between such objective location and subjective position and behaviour. Those who have faced up to this problem, for example in relation to trade union membership (e.g. Crompton, 1976), have found it difficult to specify the nature of the relationship. Another basis has been to incorporate political and ideological elements (e.g. Poulantzas, 1975), but this is subject to criticism from the other direction. That is, it gives too much weight to subjective elements and too little to objective position. (For a fuller discussion of these points see Holmwood and Stewart, 1981.)

The problem of integrating objective circumstances with the consciousness and behaviour that go with it has not been satisfactorily solved by Marxist writers. While recognising some of the strengths of the latter's position, others have found it necessary to modify it considerably, and in particular to place more emphasis on subjective factors in class formation. The most thorough-going example of this is the work of Giddens (1973) and it will be useful to consider his argument in order to help locate our own position in relation to previous accounts. He has tried to place class analysis within a broader theoretical framework which emphasises the way in which social structure is constantly being reproduced, and to some extent modified, through social action. Thus, class structure arises out of the reproduction of structuration, and 'the features of class structure [are] routinely drawn upon by actors in the course of constituting class relations as interactions; in drawing on them as modalities of interaction, they also reproduce them *as* that structure' (Giddens, 1976, 123).

However, despite his stress on action, Giddens does not develop this line of argument, instead seeing 'the major problems in the theory of class' as concerning 'the structuration of class relationships', in which is involved 'the formation of classes as identifiable social groupings'. He formulates a general three-class model for capitalist societies – upper, middle and lower – defined not merely in a formal way, but manifest in the formation of common patterns of behaviour and attitude. As determinants of such groupings he includes first, as proximate structuration, the division of labour in the productive enterprise, authority relationships and 'distributive groupings' (especially neighbourhood segregation). Secondly, he includes mediate structuration, primarily mobility chances: thus 'the structuration of classes is facilitated to the degree to which mobility closure exists'.

Unfortunately, in his analysis Giddens does not pursue his own theoretical perspective sufficiently thoroughly. That is to say, both mediate and proximate structuration are largely developed from the point of view of structure, and not from the point of view of reproduction. So he has very little to say about the behaviour of actors and groups of actors which both maintain and, to an extent, change the structure. As we shall argue later, this is in large part a result of the fact that he misunderstands the nature of the system and thus the behaviour of classes which is relevant to that system.

Another author, whose work does deal more directly with such behaviour and whose emphasis is close to our own, is Parkin (1979). He concentrates on modes of social closure as means by which groups maintain a privileged position or react to such closure on the part of others. However, his failure is to a large extent the opposite of that of Giddens, for whereas the latter places too much emphasis on the structure, Parkin places too little. His account of social closure is largely of practices which occur within a system of rewards, and does not deal directly with the criteria for reward distribution nor with the way in which those practices serve to maintain the system. In view of the strong emphasis in his earlier work (Parkin, 1971) on the analytical distinction between the structure of rewards and positions, and the allocation of individuals to those positions, it is strange that he does not elaborate the relation of social closure to these two aspects. Thus, although the discussion of the role of capital does deal both with inheritance and, more significantly, the powers of 'a limited few to grant or deny general access to the means of production and the distribution of its fruits', that concerned with credentialism ('the *inflated* use of educational certificates') deals with it only 'as a means of monitoring *entry* to key positions in the division of labour'. What is lacking here, and leads to ambiguities that we refer to later, is a consideration of the way in which the hierarchy of positions in the division of labour, as well as the mechanisms by which individuals enter and move between them, constitutes a form of exclusionary closure. Thus 'credentials' only serve as criteria of entry within the context of a particular set of criteria by which occupational tasks are determined and rewards distributed. Moreover it is far from clear that credentialism, as such, operates as significantly in the area, for example, of industrial management as it does in more bureaucratised settings.

Since Parkin is mainly concerned with processes of social closure he does not find it necessary to concentrate on the delineation of social classes. This represents a substantial advance from his earlier position which placed considerable emphasis on the manual/non-manual dividing line. Whereas previously he associated the 'dominant' class with non-manual workers and the 'subordinate' class with manual, he now, despite his disavowal of Marxist ideas, allows much greater weight to the ownership of capital. Thus he raises his major line of division to one which separates from the remainder the owners of capital and of major qualifications. However, Parkin's failure is in relating his two types of strategy to processes of the system. Thus he offers no convincing explanation of the determinants of the adoption of each strategy, arguing simply that non-manual groups tend to place 'reliance upon exclusion devices of a credentialist kind'. The reason for this is, as we suggested above, that he does not adequately fit this or his other strategies into a coherent set of understandings and practices.

In order to see why Parkin and Giddens both distinguish between social structures and the behaviour of individuals and groups within those structures, yet fail to develop a satisfactory relationship between action and structure, it is necessary to go back to the starting point of their analyses of class. For both this is Weber's original critique of Marx. Interestingly, their emphasis has been not on Weber's ideas concerning status groups as a more subjective element relating to the distribution of social honour (the difficulties involved in which have been pointed out by, e.g., Ingham, 1970b and Jones, 1975) but on his restatement of the concept of class. By agreeing that '"property" and "lack of property" are ... the basic categories of all class situations', Weber intended to make clear his acceptance of Marx's central arguments, but his understanding of the latter led him in a very different direction. Simply by taking the step of recognising the variable nature of forms of property, and of marketable skills among the propertyless, he transforms two major classes into a potential myriad of them. As we have said, both writers wish to avoid this line, but to use Weber's arguments as a means of distinguishing a small number of classes. Nonetheless, both emphasise the importance of the market for labour power. Thus, according to Giddens, 'Marx failed to recognise the potential significance of differentiations of market capacity which do not derive directly from the fact of property ownership. Such differentiations, it seems clear, are contingent upon the scarcity value of what the individual "owns" and is able to offer in the market' (1973, 103). Similarly, for Parkin 'it is the degree of scarcity relative to demand which largely determines occupational reward' (1971, 21).

Both authors, it must be said, are at the least ambivalent about the role of the market. Giddens recognises that it is not a necessary institution, in so far as its workings are considerably modified in state socialist societies, but neither he nor Parkin is clear about the status of the inequalities created by the market in capitalist societies. The latter, for example, early on stresses the primacy of market forces over convention with a quotation from an economist (Phelps-Brown), but later goes on to speak of 'the "laws" of supply and demand', suggesting by the use of inverted commas that it is convention which leaves rewards to the market. Moreover he elsewhere apparently recognises the conventional nature of market forces, pointing out that 'the fact that market principles, rather than some *other* set of criteria, are legitimised as the main determinants of rewards, is not, of course, unrelated to the fact that dominant class occupations are themselves well placed in the market'.

Whilst it is correct, virtually by definition, to argue that the existence of a market for labour will mean that there will be certain groups who will be relatively privileged when compared with others, and that therefore they have an interest in the preservation of market principles, this is not satisfactory as an explanation of the existence of the market in the first place. However, before looking at that question directly it is useful to examine more thoroughly how the market actually works in the case of labour. The classical economist's view, which is taken over by Giddens and Parkin, is that the price of labour, like that of other commodities, is determined by supply and demand. Demand is ultimately determined by 'tastes', which are taken as an irreducible given, and supply, in the case of goods other than those which are restricted because non-reproducible, by the cost of production. At any one time these two elements will be fixed and a price determined. Thus, on this view, the distribution of occupations and earnings is also determined – a matter of technical and economic necessity. All that seems to be left as a problem for the sociologist is, as Parkin shows, to examine the way in which different groups are able to control access to positions.

Already, however, viewing such control as a problem begins to undermine the market model. On its own terms, control over supply affects the price, in this case the returns to the position, and so cannot be concerned simply with who gains 'entry'. By the fact that it is a market model it cannot be treated as equivalent to the question of whether, say, the monarch is selected by inheritance rules, combat, ballot or lottery. Restriction of supply is the conventional way of treating trade unions in economic analysis (though not by labour economists with a more empirical turn of mind). Thus, for example, unions are treated as if they were monopolists, seeking to maximise the returns of their members. Such analyses, however, do not enquire at all deeply into the nature of the 'supply' of labour. So much is admitted by a convinced economic analyst (Fisher, 1971), who not only grants that of the literature in general, 'in all, treatment of supply is conspicuous by its omission' (p. 2), but that at the time he and one other were the only ones known to him who were 'currently searching for sharper hypotheses' (p. 35). The search was thought to be necessary because 'our theory of labour supply would be of limited use in empirical study of labour markets' (p. 34).

Fisher's work is very valuable in laying bare the assumptions of the market model of labour supply. In the first place he clearly equates labour and production – 'from the viewpoint of the labour analyst, the human being is a multi-product firm' (p. 7). That is to say, human beings are potentially able to supply labour of many different forms, and in doing so they, like a firm, have to relate the level supplied to the costs incurred in production. Hence, in the second place it is necessary to specify the nature of these costs. These derive from the fact that since 'nothing we desire in life is free', 'effort is always required'. Of course, 'ease, and sleep, and all the other non-market activities we tend to compound under the heading of leisure are, on our definition forms of effort' (p. 53). Thus the costs of supplying labour of a particular kind are a result of the subjective evaluation of the effort involved set against the subjective pleasure derived from it (together with other, including financial, 'costs' incurred in training and so on). As in the precisely analogous case of consumer behaviour, the ultimate determinant of demand, so here the 'tastes' involved are taken as given. Contrary to Fisher's starting point, the distinction from the situation of the firm is, then, quite clear. Firms, as buyers or sellers, are intermediaries in the process of production/consumption. For them, supply and demand are objectively determined; for individuals, on the other hand, they are primarily subjective.

Even with a market model one is led very quickly to considering the possibility, at the very least, that the 'tastes' involved in the supply of labour may be socially determined and systematically distributed. Sociologists have clearly demonstrated the existence of socially structured constraints on educational attainment and job selection, for example. Moreover, the pure market model is far from being widely accepted by economists. The idea of non-competing groups of labour was an early modification, and more recently there have developed various conceptions of segmented labour markets. In all cases the assumption of open competition is loosened or abandoned. The most substantial study of long-term changes in incomes in Britain (Routh, 1980) concludes that 'if demand and supply are at work, their influence is but dimly discerned' (p. 208) and that, certainly within employing organisations, what we witness is 'the assertion of sentiments and beliefs, hopes and convictions, of what is right and proper, just and fair, with the meting out of some sort of rough justice' (p. 219).

At the level of theoretical analysis, then, there is considerable doubt about the applicability of the market model to the determination of the returns to labour. Hence there must also be doubt about any neo-Weberian attempt to treat market capacity as a source of stratification. This is not necessarily to deny the importance of what appears as 'market capacity', but rather to emphasise the need to treat 'the labour market' in the context of overall social processes. The supply of labour is unlike the supply of any other commodity, because it is not produced under conditions similar to other commodities, and because the costs of its production are to a substantial extent socially determined. (Since our main concern has been with classical economics, it is as well to point out here that similar problems arise for Marxist analyses which stress the reproduction cost of labour.) The view of labour as a commodity is frequently criticised on moral grounds, but our argument is that it is wrong on theoretical ones.

The theoretical issue, we believe, has its counterpart in practical understanding, where again it is often mingled with moral argument. There can be little doubt about the ideological significance of the market model in accounting for differences in earnings, and elements of it are almost certainly widely diffused in popular thinking. Thus it is important, first, to consider why the market model should have the significance that it does, and how it fits in with other major organising principles of society. Secondly, it is important to see how and why the market model should persist. Central to this issue is the question of the reproduction of practices which help make the social world comprehensible, to some, in terms of this model. Thirdly, we need to look at practical problems which are thrown up for certain members of society, and the way in which these encourage actions serving to change existing practices.

The starting point for a consideration of these issues must be the market as a defining, structural feature of capitalist society. The formal exchange of equivalents provides the central dynamics of capitalism and its ideological and cognitive underpinning. Failure to see this point misled Weber in his interpretation of Marx. For the latter, the special feature of capitalism was not so much that it represented a particular form of property and thus class relationships, based upon the labour market, but that class relationships had their most developed form because they were also market relationships. One cannot, that is, first take the market as given and only then consider classes as deriving from it. The existence of a market, with labour treated as a commodity, is itself a feature of class society. Hence, while class action includes behaviour within the market, it also involves that which is concerned either with upholding or with questioning market principles.

Those who derive relative privilege from the operation of the market are of course those most likely to believe in its principles, not merely from a 'value' or 'interest' position, that they benefit, but from a cognitive viewpoint – that is, that they accept that the concept of a market is of explanatory value in accounting for distribution. Their behaviour, therefore, will be in accordance with this understanding and it follows that, somewhat paradoxically, class action on their part will be individualistic in nature. Their interests, as they understand them, in terms of this cognitive scheme, lie in maintaining the market system and in opposing attempts to introduce non-market criteria into the allocation of rewards.

This collective interest emphasises their individual interests, which are in using what they see as the laws of supply and demand by accruing qualifications, expertise or other skills desired by actual or potential employers. This point needs to be emphasised because this individualistic strategy assumes not only present relative privilege but future increase in rewards. The idea of, and belief in, the reality of a progression to better positions is built into the strategy and belief system. So also, of course, is the idea that they deserve a return to their relatively scarce skills or expertise, a belief which is buttressed by their experience, but which also serves to guide their action in such a way as, overall, to reproduce that experience.

Just as the strategies of the relatively privileged have to be seen in terms of the organising principles of capitalist society, especially the market, so also do the strategies of the less privileged, the social closure by usurpation in Parkin's terms. These overwhelmingly are collectivist in nature, in contrast to the individualistic strategies of the privileged. However it is not this which distinguishes them, nor is it that they are forms of 'usurpation', but the fact that to a greater or lesser extent they tend to deny market principles of allocation and seek to establish other criteria. We believe that this can have significant implications for the development of social change. However, arguments in relation to this need to be set within a broader context, particularly that of a discussion of the nature of trade unionism. For that reason the argument will not be developed at length here, but left to the volume specifically devoted to that topic.

The problems of the operation of market principles, and therefore of class relations, are not, of course, generated and acted out only in the sphere of collective attempts to modify work rewards. Indeed to a large extent common interests are generated by social processes which also create problems for the market model in other respects. For example, the public sector in our work is the most highly organised in terms of unionism and collective identification, but it challenges a market model in a much more fundamental way. The very existence of a large service sector, governmental or otherwise, has caused increasing problems for market models, both capitalist and Marxist. On the one hand conservative theories of wages and of production have failed in this area and have been replaced, practically, by arguments about 'equivalence'. On the other, since Marx assumed that the service sector would always be small and dependent upon the overwhelming power of the capitalist, modern Marxists have had to produce new explanations to account for the massive growth in this area. For the most part they have done this by *ad hoc* modifications of the basic theory which in their implications have undermined its central tenets. We need new integrated explanations which can account for the collective character of the social and economic organisation of modern societies. In the process 'class' analysis, bound as it is to market principles, will be transformed.

However, the concern in our present research with adaptations to employment situations can be clearly linked to more general 'class' issues. Adaptations are related both to forms of social closure, in terms either of exclusion or usurpation, and also to questions of reproduction of the social system. We believe that it is important to stress the relationship of adaptations to principles of social organisation, particularly the question of the operation of market criteria. Social class is essentially bound up with the existence of a market-based society, and therefore class action is essentially concerned with the role of the market. This is not simply a question of conflict *within* the market, but more importantly of conflict *about* the market.

It is clear that our concern is with changes occurring within capitalist society, and not with the question of its revolutionary over-throw. Our emphasis on the cognitive element makes it possible both to allow for non-revolutionary change and to relate this in an intelligible way to action based upon existing forms of understanding. That is to say, rather than looking – or looking only – for full-blown class consciousness, it might be useful to consider the practical difficulties that face some groups within their present understanding of their society. Their attempts to come to terms with practical and immediate problems, bearing in mind that a problem is such only within a particular cognitive scheme, may then be seen as contributing both to the reproduction of the existing structure and also to its expanded reproduction, in the sense of 'regular social processes, intelligible in terms of current knowledge, which have the practical consequences of transforming social arrangements in consistent directions' (Stewart, Prandy and Blackburn, 1980, 277). One aspect of such reproduction is the development of cognitions themselves, both in reaction to the changed nature of experience, and as a basis for further changes.

It is in the light of such ideas that we see our work on adaptations and their relationship to expectations, perceptions and so on. Depending on their circumstances, some groups of individuals will have expectations with respect to certain rewards that are not being met. This 'problem', which occurs within their current understanding, requires a solution which, to a greater or lesser extent, will be one that is also available within that understanding. Those that are in large part consistent with it, such as the individualistic pursuit of promotion, will mainly function to bring about simple reproduction. Some, such as psychological withdrawal, may do little directly to bring about a change, although problems may occur in other parts of the system if they are widespread. Finally, there are solutions such as collective bargaining, whose consequences may involve changing the system though not necessarily always in the way intended by those who adopt them.

Thus we have moved from the question of 'class' back to our general theoretical model, and the circle is complete. We have tried to show how that model can be accommodated to an emphasis on social processes and so to demonstrate the interconnectedness of individual experience and social reproduction. However adequate or inadequate the present attempt may be judged to be in relation to the problems to which it addresses itself, we believe this to be the vital theoretical problem.

Appendix I
Individual Interview
Schedule and Checklist

(a) INTERVIEW SCHEDULE

To begin with I should like a few details about your education and occupational experience.
1. Which school did you last attend?
   What type of school was that?
   (a) Grammar
       Direct Grant
       Senior Secondary (Scot.)
   (b) Secondary Modern
       Junior Secondary (Scot.)
   (c) Public
   (d) Private
   (e) Technical
   (f) Comprehensive
   (g) Elementary
       Senior
   (h) Central
       Intermediate
   (i) Other
       (specify)
   (j) Foreign
       (specify)
2. How old were you when you left this school?
3. At the time that you left school what was your father's occupation?
   Please ensure respondent is as specific as possible; note the industry where necessary. If several occupations, ask about main one; if during wartime (or father retired or dead) record and ask for former occupation.
   Manual
   Skilled/qualified
   Supervisory
   Self-employed
4. Is, or was your father ever, a member of a trade union?
5. Have you had any further education since leaving school?

Was it full-time or part-time?

How many years did you have?

6. Do you have any qualifications?

    If yes: What are they?

    (a) Degree: science/technology

    (b) Degree: other

    (c) Professional institution

    (d) HNC

    (e) C&G $\left.\begin{matrix} \\ \\ \\ \end{matrix}\right\}$ science
         ONC   technology
         A-level

    (f) C&G $\left.\begin{matrix} \\ \\ \\ \end{matrix}\right\}$ commercial
         ONC
         A-level

    (g) Minor qualifications: technical

    (h) Minor qualifications: commercial

    (i) General qualifications

    (j) None

7. What was your first full-time job?

    Ensure that respondent is specific. Note the industry where necessary.

8. When did you join this firm?

9. What was your first job here?

10. When did you start your present job

11. What is your date of birth?

12. Are you married?

    Other: widowed, divorced, separated.

13. Do you have any children?

    If yes: How many are still dependent on you?

14. Do you have any other dependents?

    Apart from wife and children.

15. What is your basic gross income?

16. Do you earn any extra?

    If yes: How much (net)?

17. Are there any other members of your household working?

    If yes: How much altogether do they earn (net)?

18. Whereabouts did you live for most of your childhood?

    Write in name of town, or nearest town or village, and country.

19. How often have you moved house since getting your first job?

    Apart from local moves.

20. Where do you live now?

    Do you rent or own your home?

    If rented: Is it rented privately or from a council?

21. Can you tell me what are the occupations of your four nearest neighbours?

    Note whether self-employed and the industry, where this will help to make clear the nature of an occupation.

22. Do you belong to any associations (clubs, churches, etc.) not concerned with work?

    If yes: For each association: About how frequently do you attend?

23. Can you think of four people with whom you are friendly outside work. What are their occupations?

> *Prompt for four occupations other than that of respondent. Note industry and whether self-employed.*
>
> *As respondent gives each occupation ask:*
>> (a) Does he work in this establishment?
>> (a) Is he a relative?

I should now like to ask a few questions on the number of people you work with, and so on.

24. How many people are there in the same room as you are in, including yourself?

> *Room includes open offices.*

25. How many people of about your own level are there under the same immediate superior as you, including yourself?

In the next two questions by work-group we mean people in the immediate geographical area with whom the respondent regularly interacts.

26. How many people are there in your work-group doing jobs similar to your own, including yourself?

27. How many people are there in your work-group with similar qualifications (or experience) to your own, including yourself?

Considering a normal working day for you, for example yesterday (or last working day):

28.   (a) How many of your superiors did you see to talk to?
       (b) How long altogether did this take?

29.   (a) How many of your subordinates did you see to talk to?
       (b) How long altogether did this take?

30.   (a) How many other people did you see to talk to?
       (b) How long altogether did this take?

31. You have already given us information on several aspects of your job. No-one has a perfect job, and almost everyone could think of ways in which his job could be improved. Some improvements would obviously be more important than others. On these cards are various aspects of a job that other people have considered to be important. If a small improvement in any one of these were possible, which one would you most want it to be?

> Which would be next most important to you?
>
> Please continue choosing the cards in order of importance.
>
> *Ensure that respondent orders all cards.*

32. This question is similar to the last except that the statements on the cards are about collective representation – consultation machinery, trade unions and so on.

> (a) Could you first of all look carefully through and divide them into those that, on the whole, you agree with and those you disagree with?
>
> (b) Taking those with which you agree choose the one that you agree with most, put it on top of the pile and arrange the others in the order that you agree with them.

    (c)   Do the same with those you disagree with, putting the one with which you least disagree to the top of the pile.

    (d)   Put the two piles together and check that the statements are in the order that you agree with them.

Now read out the statements starting with that with which you most agree.

Draw a line to divide statements with which respondents agree from statements with which they disagree.

(b) CHECKLIST

JOB TITLE:
   Brief description of duties:

SECTION I

The following items are concerned with the people that you work with.

Jobs are different in the extent to which they allow people to talk with one another while working. Tick the statement which *best* describes your job.
   My job *very rarely* allows me to talk to other people at all.
   My job *seldom* allows me to talk to other people.
   My job *sometimes* allows me to talk to other people.
   My job *often* allows me to talk to other people.
   My job allows me to talk to other people *very often*.

Is your answer to the previous question a reason for liking or disliking your job?

   It is a strong reason for liking my job.
   It is a reason for liking my job, but not very important.
   I just feel neutral about this.
   It is a reason for disliking my job, but not too important.
   It is a strong reason for disliking my job.

Do you feel that people who work with you form a team?

   Yes, I do feel that people who work with me form a strong team.
   Yes, there is quite a bit of team spirit.
   There is some team spirit.
   There is very little team spirit.
   No, I do not feel that people who work with me form a team at all.

How do you think that your group compares with other groups in the way that people stick together and help each other?

   Much less helpful than other groups.
   Somewhat less helpful.
   About the same.
   Somewhat more helpful.
   Much more helpful.

Thinking *only* of the people that you work with, and ignoring all other aspects of your job, would you indicate with an 'X' where you would place yourself on the line below.

Below are a number of statements about your *immediate superior*. Could you put a tick in the appropriate box to indicate how much you agree or disagree with each statement.

> He is much more helpful than others.
> He does not tell me where I stand.
> He knows his job well.
> He seldom praises good work.
> He often asks my advice.
> He stands up for his staff.

Please tick the statement which *best* describes how well you get on with your immediate superior.

> Not at all well.
> Not too well.
> Fairly well.
> Very well.
> Extremely well.

Is your answer to the previous question a reason for liking or disliking your job?

> It is a strong reason for liking my job.
> It is a reason for liking my job, but not very important.
> I just feel neutral about this.
> It is a reason for disliking my job, but not too important.
> It is a strong reason for disliking my job.

Thinking *only* of your immediate superior, and ignoring all other aspects of your job, would you indicate with an 'X' where you would place yourself on the line below.

SECTION II

The next few items deal with how you view the security of your job.

How would you rate the security of your job, compared with the following?

> (a) the average manual worker (Please put an 'X' on the line);
> (b) the average top manager;
> (c) the average person doing, broadly, your type of work.

Do you think your job ought to be: (much more secure – much less secure)

As far as security of employment alone is concerned, and ignoring all other aspects of your job, would you indicate with an 'X' where you would place yourself on the line below.

SECTION III

Below are a number of statements about the work that you actually do. Could you put a tick in the appropriate box to indicate how much you agree or disagree with each statement.

A person who wanted to make his own decisions would be discouraged here.

Anyone with reasonable qualifications could learn to do my job within about one month.

My job provides me with excellent opportunities to increase my knowledge and abilities.

I am completely free to organise my work as I want to.

My job uses only a small part of my abilities.

I feel that I am my own boss in most matters.

I almost always do the same thing in my job; there is hardly any variety.

I feel that I am doing an exceptionally worthwhile job here.

I should be happier if I had more responsibility.

I should like to be able to use more of my own ideas on this job.

The company ought to do more to allow people to increase their knowledge and abilities.

My job ought to be much more varied than it is.

I would sometimes welcome more guidance from my superior.

Thinking only of the actual work that you do, and ignoring all other aspects of your job, would you indicate where you would place yourself on the line below.

SECTION IV

Occupations differ in the amount of prestige or social standing that they have, and we should like your views on this, considering your own occupation in relation to manual workers and top managers. Because there may be differences, we have made a distinction between standing in the community at large and within this company.

Thinking first in terms only of the community at large, whereabouts on the line below do you think that your job

(a) is placed by other people?
   Indicate with an arrow from above
(b) ought to be placed?
   Indicate with an arrow from below

Now thinking only of this company, whereabouts on the line below do you think that your job

(a) is placed by other people?
   Indicate with an arrow from above
(b) ought to be placed?
   Indicate with an arrow from below

Thinking only of the general standing and prestige aspects, and ignoring all other aspects of your job, would you indicate where you would place yourself on the line below.

SECTION V

Income: the following two questions ask for (a) your estimates of what the income of certain groups *is*, and (b) what you think their income *ought to be*, taking all things into consideration. As before, we have distinguished between this country in general and this company.

Thinking first of people generally in *this country*, what would you say:
    (a) IS
    (b) OUGHT TO BE
        the gross weekly earnings (before deductions) of an average manual worker;
        the annual salary of an average top manager;
        the average annual salary of a man of your age doing, broadly, your type of work.

Thinking now of people employed in this company what would you say:
    (a) IS
    (b) OUGHT TO BE
        the gross weekly earnings (before deductions) of an average manual worker;
        the annual salary of an average top manager;
        the average annual salary of a man of your age doing, broadly, your type of work.

Now we should like to know how satisfied you are with your own earnings.

Only so far as the money is concerned, and ignoring all other aspects of your job, would you indicate where you would place yourself on the line below.

SECTION VI

Below are a number of statements about promotion. Could you put a tick in the appropriate box to indicate how much you agree or disagree with each statement.

In this job I have excellent chances of getting ahead in comparison with other lines of work.
Promotion comes slowly in this company.
It is not always the best people who are chosen for promotion in this company.
There are many good opportunities for me outside this company.
Chances of getting on in this job are much better than could be reasonably expected.
This job ought to provide much better opportunities for getting ahead.
I would not let friendship ties stand in the way of moving on to a better job.

I prefer a steady job to taking a chance on one that might lead to promotion.

I would rather take a job with long-term prospects than one paying a high salary.

I wouldn't take a promotion, no matter how big an improvement it was for me, if it meant that I might endanger my health.

Most people are determined to get ahead in their job.

I really prefer to put my roots down somewhere, rather than move as the chances for advancement come along.

Thinking only of your chances of getting ahead in your present job, and ignoring all other aspects of it, could you indicate where you would place yourself on the line below.

SECTION VII

Now we should like you to think of your job as a whole. Could you first tick each of the following statements to indicate how much, all things considered, you agree or disagree with it.

Sometimes it is not really worthwhile working hard at my job.

I get highly involved in my work and put in a great deal of effort.

I sometimes feel that I would prefer not to come to work.

I would leave this job at once if I had another to go to.

Even if I came into a great deal of money I would still continue to work.

I have been seriously considering moving to another job.

I have found that in order to get along at work you usually have to put on an act instead of being able to be your real self.

What others think I should do is usually not what I would really like to do.

I frequently have to do things to please others that I would rather not do.

When I'm with other people, I try to keep in mind that saying what you really feel often gets you into trouble.

I have found that rules more often than not go against human nature.

I have found that just being your natural self won't get you very far in your job.

Sometimes I get restless because I can't express my real feelings when talking and doing things with others.

Taking into account ALL aspects of your job, could you indicate where you would place yourself on the line below.

Appendix II
The Calculation of 'Expectations' from Perceptions and Gaps

Given two measures on the one hand of perceptions, and on the other of the gap between 'expectations' and 'perceptions', it would appear to follow that:

expectations (X) = 'expectations' (X) − 'perceptions' (Z) + perceptions (Z), i.e. gap (Y) added to perceptions (Z).

However this assumes that 'perceptions' are measured in the same units as perceptions. In fact we have:

$$Z' = \text{perceptions}$$

and

$$Y = X - Z,$$

where X and Z are not directly measured, and the problem is to convert Z' and Z to the same units in order to be able to estimate X.

One solution might be to regress Y on Z' to obtain the necessary weighting. Unfortunately this would leave an estimate of X completely independent of Z (i.e. $r_{xz} = 0$), which we know to be empirically unrealistic (from the cases of income and status). This leads to the clearer formulation, where $X = f(Z)$ so that:

$$Y = f(Z) - Z$$

and we wish to estimate $f(Z)$. That is, we wish to remove some, but not all, of Z from Y. The amount that we remove depends on the value chosen for r_{xz}. To a certain extent this decision is arbitrary, though we shall offer a justification for a particular choice later.

The relationships between the measures can be summarised in a path diagram (Figure A.1), where x, z and y represent the three variables in standardised form, with y entirely determined by x and z, and the problem

FIGURE A.1

201

now is to determine p_{yx} and p_{yz}. We have overcome the difficulty of units of measurement, partly, by converting variables to standardised form, so that both measures of z are the same, apart from a constant. We can safely ignore the constant as it is reasonable to suppose Z and Z' have the same zero and, more fundamentally, because if it is not zero it merely alters the zero point of X. However, we now have to make an assumption to reduce the number of unknowns. Rather than choose an arbitrary value for r_{xz} we can do this by defining the ratio of the variances of X and Z (which is effectively the same thing). Since they are the two components of the perception Y it seems reasonable to suppose they have equal variances, and in this sense contribute equally to Y^*. So:

$$S_X = S_Z$$

$$y = (S_x/S_y)(x-z), \text{ from } Y = X - Z \text{ so that } yS_Y = xS_X - zS_Z$$

path $\qquad p_{yx} = -p_{yz}$

and $\qquad r_{xy} = -r_{zy}$

Thus

$$r_{yz} = r_{(x-z)z} = \frac{\Sigma(xz - z^2)}{\sqrt{\Sigma(x-z)^2\Sigma z^2}} = \frac{r_{xz} - 1}{\sqrt{(2 - 2r_{xz})}} = \frac{-1}{\sqrt{2}}\sqrt{(1 - r_{xz})}$$

So $\qquad\qquad\qquad r_{xz} = 1 - 2r^2_{yz}$

By the usual path equation (only one is needed here):

$$p_{yx} + r_{xz}p_{yz} = r_{xy}$$

Substituting for p_{yz}, r_{xz} and r_{xy} gives

$$-p_{yz} + (1 - 2r^2_{yz})p_{yz} = -r_{zy}$$
$$p_{yz} = \frac{1}{2r_{zy}}$$

So $\qquad\qquad\qquad y = \frac{-1}{2r_{zy}}(x - z), \text{ since } y = p_{yz}z + p_{yz}x$

and $\qquad\qquad \frac{S_X}{S_Y} = \frac{-1}{2r_{zy}}, \text{ since } y = \frac{S_X}{S_Y}(x - z)$

Therefore, converting to unstandardised form, using Z' rather than Z.

$$Y = X - \frac{S_Y}{S_{Z'}}Z'$$

---

* In fact it is likely that there is at least as much variation in expectations as in perceptions. The assumption of equal variances implies a reasonably high correlation between the two, given the observed correlations between perceptions and gaps. However the final results from this method are of comparable levels with those from the direct measurement of expectations.

$$X = Y - \frac{S_Y}{2r_{zy}S_{z'}} Z'$$

To see how this works out in the case of intrinsic job requires consideration of an additional complication. Here we have two different perception measures, and it is desirable to combine them in some optimal way to create a single perception measure. If we again consider a path diagram (Figure A.2), where z_1 is control, and z_2 use of abilities, it is clear that one solution is to split the path p_{yz_1} into two components, where z is entirely determined by z_1 and z_2,

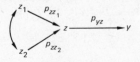

FIGURE A.2

such that $p_{yz_1} = p_{yz} \, p_{zz_1}$, and similarly for p_{yz_2}. That is we require all of the effects of z_1 and z_2 to pass through z (cf. Heise's sheaf coefficient, 1972). Then we have a unique solution. It is possible to compute p_{yz_1} and p_{yz_2} in the usual way. Then, by the normal rules of path analysis we have:

$$p_{zz_i} = p_{yz_i}/p_{yz} \qquad r_{zz_i} = r_{yz_i}/p_{yz} \qquad (i = 1, 2)$$

(bearing in mind that p_{yz} in fact includes an indirect relationship through x).

Since z is wholly determined:

$$(p_{yz_1}/p_{yz})(r_{yz_1}/p_{yz}) + (p_{yz_2}/p_{yz})(r_{yz_1}/p_{yz}) = 1$$
$$p_{yz}^2 = p_{yz_1}(p_{yz_1} + r_{z_1z_2}p_{yz_2}) + p_{yz_2}(p_{yz_2} + r_{z_1z_2}p_{yz_1})$$
$$p_{yz} = (p_{yz_1}^2 + p_{yz_2}^2 + 2\,p_{yz_1}p_{yz_2}r_{z_1z_2})^{1/2}$$

In the case of intrinsic job, this gives:

$$p_{yz} = -0.4712,$$
$$p_{zz_1} = 0.4115, \ p_{zz_2} = 0.7804$$
$$z = 0.4115\,z_1 + 0.7804\,z_2$$
$$Z = 0.4616\,Z_1 + 0.9055\,Z_2, \text{ where } S_Z = 1$$
$$X = Y - \frac{0.8414}{2(-0.4712)\,(1.0)} \ (0.4616\,Z_1 + 0.9055\,Z_2)$$
$$= Y + 0.4121\,Z_1 + 0.8085\,Z_2$$

A similar calculation for the perceptions of security gives

$$Z = 0.1699\,Z_1 + 0.4782\,Z_2 + 0.2696\,Z_3$$

where Z_1 is security compared with those at the individual's own level, Z_2 is that compared with manual workers, and Z_3 that compared with top managers. Thus also:

$$X = Y + 0.2015\,Z_1 + 0.5672\,Z_2 + 0.3197\,Z_3$$

Bibliography

Argyris, C. (1957) *Personality and Organisation* (New York: Harper).

Atkinson, J. W. (1964) *An Introduction to Motivation* (Princeton, N.J.: Van Nostrand).

Bain, G. S. (1970) *The Growth of White Collar Unionism* (Oxford University Press).

Baldamus, W. (1961) *Efficiency and Effort: An Analysis of Industrial Administration* (London: Tavistock).

Banks, J. A. (1963) *Industrial Participation* (Liverpool University Press).

Berger, P. L. and T. Luckmann, (1967) *The Social Construction of Reality* (London: Allen Lane).

Beynon, H. and R. M. Blackburn, (1972) *Perceptions of Work* (Cambridge University Press).

Birnbaum, I. (1977) 'Greater Indeterminism in Causal Analysis', *Quality and Quantity*, vol. 11, no. 2.

Blackburn, R. M. (1967) *Union Character and Social Class* (London: Batsford).

Blackburn, R. M. and M. Mann, (1979) *The Working Class in the Labour Market* (London: Macmillan).

Blackburn, R. M. and K. Prandy, (1965) 'White-Collar Unionism: A Conceptual Framework', *British Journal of Sociology*, vol. XVI, no. 2.

Blackburn, R. M., A. Stewart, and K. Prandy, (1980) 'Part-time Education and the Alternative Route', *Sociology*, vol. 14, no. 4.

Blalock, H. M. (1964) *Causal Inferences in Non-experimental Research* (Chapel Hill: University of North Carolina Press).

Blalock, H. M. (ed.) (1971) *Causal Models in Social Science* (London: Macmillan).

Blau, P. M. (1956) *Bureaucracy in Modern Society* (New York: Random House).

Blau, P. M. (1964) *Exchange and Power in Social Life* (New York: Wiley).

Blau, P. M. and W. R. Scott (1963) *Formal Organisations* (London: Routledge & Kegan Paul).

Blauner, R. (1964) *Alienation and Freedom: The Factory Worker and His Industry* (University of Chicago Press).

Bonjean, C. M., G. D. Bruce, and J. A. Williams Jnr, (1967) 'Social Mobility and Job Satisfaction: a Replication and Extension', *Social Forces*, vol. 45, no. 4.

Bonjean, C. M. and M. D. Grimes, (1970) 'Bureaucracy and Alienation: A Dimensional Approach', *Social Forces*, vol. 48, no. 3.

Carchedi, G. (1975) 'On the Economic Indentification of the New Middle Class', *Economy and Society*, vol. 4, no. 1.

Coleman, J. S. (1964) *Introduction to Mathematical Sociology* (Glencoe, Ill.: Free Press/London: Collier-Macmillan).

Coombs, C. H. (1964) *A Theory of Data* (New York: Wiley).

Crompton, R. (1976) 'Approaches to the Study of White-Collar Unionism', *Sociology*, vol. 10, no. 3.

Cunnison, S. (1966) *Wages and Work Allocation* (London: Tavistock).

DEP (1970) *Employment and Productivity Gazette* (November).

Dubin, R. (1956) 'Industrial Workers' Worlds: A Study of the "Central Life Interests" of Industrial Workers', *Social Problems*, vol. 3, no. 3.

Duncan, O. D., A. O. Haller, and A. Portes (1968) 'Peer Influences on Aspirations: A Reinterpretation', *American Journal of Sociology*, vol. 74, no. 1.

Durkheim, E. (1952) *Suicide* (London: Routledge & Kegan Paul).

Etzioni, A. (1961) *A Comparative Analysis of Complex Organisations* (Glencoe, Ill.: The Free Press).

Fisher, M. R. (1971) *The Economic Analysis of Labour* (London: Weidenfeld & Nicolson).

Form, W. H. and J. A. Geschwender, (1962) 'Social Reference Basis of Job Satisfaction: The Case of Manual Workers', *American Sociological Review*, vol. 27, no. 2.

Friedmann, E. A. and R. J. Havighurst (1954) *The Meaning of Work and Retirement* (University of Chicago Press).

Giddens, A. (1973) *The Class Structure of the Advanced Societies* (London: Hutchinson).

Giddens, A. (1976) *New Rules of Sociological Method* (London: Hutchinson).

Goldthorpe, J. H. (1966) 'Attitudes and Behaviour of Car Assembly Workers: A Deviant Case and a Theoretical Critique', *British Journal of Sociology*, vol. XVII, no. 3.

Goldthorpe, J. H. (1980) *Social Mobility and Class Structure in Modern Britain* (Oxford University Press).

Goldthorpe, J. H., D. Lockwood, F. Bechhofer, and J. Platt, (1968) *The Affluent Worker: Industrial Attitudes and Behaviour* (Cambridge University Press).

Goodman, L. A. (1959) 'Simple Statistical Methods for Scalogram Analysis', *Psychometrika*, vol. 24.

Green, B. S. A. (1956) 'A Method of Scalogram Analysis using Summary Statistics', *Psychometrika*, vol. 21.

Guttman, L. (1954) 'A New Approach to Factor Analysis: The Radex,' in P. F. Lazarsfeld, (ed.), *Mathematical Thinking in the Social Sciences* (New York: Russell & Russell).

Handy, L. J. (1968) 'Absenteeism and Attendance in the British Coal-Mining Industry: An Examination of Post-war Trends', *British Journal of Industrial Relations*, vol. VI, no. 1.

Harman, H. H. (1967) *Modern Factor Analysis* (University of Chicago Press).

Hauser, R. M. and A. S. Goldberger, (1971) 'The Treatment of Unobservable Variables in Path Analysis,' in H. L. Costner (ed.), *Sociological Methodology 1971* (San Francisco: Jossey-Bass).

Heise, D. R. (1969) 'Problems in Path Analysis and Causal Inference', in E. F. Borgatta (ed.), *Sociological Methodology 1969* (San Francisco: Jossey-Bass).

Heise, D. R. (1972) 'Employing Nominal Variables, Induced Variables and Block Variables in Path Analysis, *Sociological Methods and Research*, vol. 1, no. 2.

Herzberg, F. (1968) *Work and the Nature of Man* (London: Staples Press).

Holmwood, J. M. and A. Stewart, (1981) 'The Role of Contradiction in Modern Theories of Social Stratification' (mimeo: paper presented at BSA Conference, April).

Horton, J. (1964) 'The Dehumanisation of Anomie and Alienation', *British Journal of Sociology*, vol. xv, no. 4.

Ingham, G. K. (1970a) *Size of Industrial Organization and Worker Behaviour* (Cambridge University Press).

Ingham, G. K. (1970b) 'Social Stratification: Individual Attributes and Social Relationships', *Sociology*, vol. 4, no. 1.

Johnston, J. (1963) *Econometric Methods* (New York: McGraw-Hill).

Jones, B. (1975) 'Max Weber and the Concept of Social Class', *Sociological Review*, vol. 23, no. 4.

Kerr, C. and A. Siegel, (1954) 'The Inter-Industry Propensity to Strike', in W. Kornhauser, R. Dubin and A. M. Ross (eds), *Industrial Conflict* (New York: McGraw-Hill).

Kohn, M. L. (1969) *Class and Conformity* (Homewood, Ill.: Dorsey Press).

Kompass – United Kingdom (1968), Register of British Industry and Commerce, vol. 3, Company Information (in association with Confederation of British Industry).

Kornhauser, A. (1965) *Mental Health of the Industrial Worker* (New York: Wiley).

Labovitz, S. (1970) 'The Assignment of Numbers to Rank Order Categories', *American Sociological Review*, vol. 35, no. 3.

Land, K. C. (1969) 'Principles of Path Analysis', in E. F. Borgatta (ed.), *Sociological Methodology 1969* (San Francisco: Jossey-Bass).

Lazarsfeld, P. F. (1959) 'Problems in Methodology', in R. K. Merton, L. Broom and L. S. Cottrell (eds), *Sociology Today* (New York: Basic Books).

Lazarsfeld, P. F. and N. W. Henry (1968) *Latent Structure Analysis* (Boston: Houghton Mifflin).

Lazarsfeld, P. E. and H. Menzel, (1961) 'On the Relation Between Individual and Collective Properties', in A. Etzioni (ed.), *Complex Organisations: A Sociological Reader* (New York: Holt, Reinhart & Winston).

Lee, D. J. (1966) 'Industrial Training and Social Class', *Sociological Review*, vol. 14, no. 3.

Lipset, S. M. and M. Trow (1957) 'Reference Group Theory and Trade Union Wage Policy', in M. Komarovsky (ed.), *Common Frontiers of the Social Sciences* (Glencoe, Ill.: The Free Press).

Lipset, S. M., M. A. Trow, and J. S. Coleman, (1956) *Union Democracy: The Internal Politics of the International Typographical Union* (Glencoe, Ill.: The Free Press).

Lockwood, D. (1958) *The Blackcoated Worker* (London: Allen & Unwin).
Lord, F. M. (1963) 'Biserial Estimates of Correlation', *Psychometrika*, vol. 28.
Lupton, T. (1963) *On the Shop Floor* (London: Pergamon).
Marshall, A. (1920) *Principles of Economics* (8th edn) (London: Macmillan).
Marx, K. (1961) *Economic and Philosophic Manuscripts of 1844* (Moscow: Foreign Languages Publishing House).
Maslow, A. H. (1954) *Motivation and Personality* (New York: Harper).
Mayo, E. (1945) *The Social Problems of an Industrial Civilization* (Boston: Graduate School of Business Administration, Harvard University).
Merton, R. K. (1957) *Social Theory and Social Structure* (Glencoe, Ill.: Free Press).
Merton, R. K. and A. Kitt, (1952) 'Contributions to the Theory of Reference Group Behaviour' in G. Swanson, S. Newcomb and C. Hartley (eds), *Readings in Social Psychology* (New York: Holt).
Mészáros, I. (1970) *Marx's Theory of Alienation* (London: Merlin).
Morse, N. C. and R. S. Weiss, (1955) 'The Function and Meaning of Work and the Job', *American Sociological Review*, vol. 20, no. 2.
Neal, A. G. and S. Rettig, (1963) 'Dimensions of Alienation Among Manual and Non-Manual Workers, *American Sociological Review*, vol. 28, no. 4.
Nettler, G., 'A Measure of Alienation', *American Sociological Review*, vol. 22, no. 6.
Nie, N. H., C. H. Hull, J. G. Jenkins, K. Steinbrenner and D. H. Bent (1975) *SPSS: Statistical Package for the Social Sciences* (New York: McGraw-Hill).
Ollman, B. (1971) *Alienation: Marx's Conception of Man in Capitalist Society* (Cambridge University Press).
Palmer, G. L., H. S. Parnes, R. C. Wilcock, M. W. Herman and C. P. Brainerd (1962) *The Reluctant Job Changer* (Philadelphia: University of Pennsylvania Press).
Parkin, F. (1971) *Class Inequality and Political Order* (London: MacGibbon & Kee).
Parkin, F. (1979) *Marxism and Class Theory: A Bourgeois Critique* (London: Tavistock).
Patchen, M. (1968) 'The Effect of Reference Group Standards on Job Satisfaction', in H. H. Hyman and E. Singer (eds), *Readings in Reference Group Theory and Research* (New York: The Free Press).
Portes, A. (1971) 'On the Interpretation of Class Consciousness', *American Journal of Sociology*, vol. 77, no. 2.
Poulantzas, N. (1975) *Classes in Contemporary Capitalism* (London: New Left Books).
Prandy, K. (1965a) *Professional Employees* (London: Faber & Faber).
Prandy, K. (1965b) 'Professional Organisation in Great Britain', *Industrial Relations*, vol. 5, no. 1.
Prandy, K. (1979) 'Alienation and Interests in the Analysis of Social Cognitions', *British Journal of Sociology*, vol. XXX, no. 4.

Prandy, K., A. Stewart and R. M. Blackburn, (1974) 'Concepts and Measures: The Example of Unionateness', *Sociology*, vol. 8, no. 3.

Quinn, R. P. and T. W. Mangione, (1973) 'Evaluating Weighted Models of Measuring Job Satisfaction: a Cinderella Story', *Organisational Behaviour and Human Performance*, vol. 10, no. 1.

Raffe, D. (1979) 'The "Alternative Route" Reconsidered: Part-time Further Education and Social Mobility in England and Wales', *Sociology*, vol. 13, no. 1.

Roethlisberger, F. J. and W. J. Dickson (1939) *Management and the Worker* (Harvard University Press).

Rose, D. (1972) 'Some Sociological Aspects of Rural Industrialisation' (unpublished).

Roskam, E. E. (1969) *Metric Analysis of Ordinal Data in Psychology* (Amsterdam: Vam-Voorschoten).

Routh, G. (1980) *Occupation and Pay in Great Britain 1906-79* (London: Macmillan).

Sayles, L. R. (1958) *Behavior of Industrial Work Groups: Prediction and Control* (New York: Wiley).

Schooler, C. (1968) 'A Note of Extreme Caution on the Use of Guttman Scales', *American Journal of Sociology*, vol. 74, no. 3.

Scott, W. H., J. A. Banks, A. H. Halsey and T. Lupton (1956) *Technical Change and Industrial Relations* (Liverpool University Press).

Seeman, M. (1958) 'Social Mobility and Administrative Behaviour', *American Sociological Review*, vol. 23, no. 6.

Seeman, M. (1959) 'On the Meaning of Alienation', *American Sociological Review*, vol. 24, no. 6.

Silverman, D. (1968) 'Formal Organisations or Industrial Sociology: Towards a Social Action Analysis of Organizations', *Sociology*, vol. 2, no. 2.

Smith, P. C., L. M. Kendal, and C. L. Hulin (1969) *The Measurement of Satisfaction in Work and Retirement* (Chicago: Rand McNally).

Spinrad, W. (1960) 'Correlates of Trade Union Participation: A Summary of the Literature', *American Sociological Review*, vol. 25, no. 2.

Stewart, A. and R. M. Blackburn, (1975) 'The Stability of Structural Inequality', *Sociological Review*, vol. 23, no. 3.

Stewart, A., K. Prandy, and R. M. Blackburn (1980) *Social Stratification and Occupations* (London: Macmillan).

Sykes, A. J. M. (1965) 'Some Differences in the Attitudes of Clerical and of Manual Workers', *Sociological Review*, vol. 13, no. 1.

Taylor, F. W. (1947) *The Principles of Scientific Management,* in *Scientific Management* (New York: Harper).

Turner, A. N. and P. R. Lawrence (1965) *Industrial Jobs and the Worker* (Boston: Division of Research, Harvard Business School).

Whyte, W. F. (1955) *Money and Motivation* (New York: Harper & Row).

Willer, D. (1967) *Scientific Sociology: Theory and Method* (New Jersey: Prentice-Hall).

Wright, E. O. (1976) 'Class Boundaries in Advanced Capitalist Societies', *New Left Review*, vol. 98.

Wright, E. O. (1978) 'Race, Class and Income Inequality' *American Journal of Sociology*, vol. 83, no. 6.
Wright, E. O. (1979) *Class Structure and Income Determination* (New York: Academic Press).
Zaleznik, A., C. R. Christensen and F. J. Roethlisberger, (1958) *The Motivation, Productivity and Satisfaction of Workers: A Prediction Study* (Boston: Graduate School of Business Administration, Harvard University).
Zetterberg, H. L. (1962) *Social Theory and Social Practice* (New York: Bedminster Press).

Index